W9-BFP-255

Social Reach

A Connectivist Approach to American Identity and Global Governance

Tian-jia Dong

University Press of America,® Inc.
Lanham • Boulder • New York • Toronto • Plymouth, UK

Copyright © 2008 by
University Press of America,® Inc.
4501 Forbes Boulevard
Suite 200
Lanham, Maryland 20706
UPA Acquisitions Department (301) 459-3366

Estover Road
Plymouth PL6 7PY
United Kingdom

All rights reserved
Printed in the United States of America
British Library Cataloging in Publication Information Available

Library of Congress Control Number: 2008923605
ISBN-13: 978-0-7618-4056-5 (clothbound : alk. paper)
ISBN-10: 0-7618-4056-7 (clothbound : alk. paper)
ISBN-13: 978-0-7618-4057-2 (paperback : alk. paper)
ISBN-10: 0-7618-4057-5 (paperback : alk. paper)

∞™ The paper used in this publication meets the minimum
requirements of American National Standard for Information
Sciences—Permanence of Paper for Printed Library Materials,
ANSI Z39.48—1984

Contents

Preface and Acknowledgments

This book is about constructing the identity of global leadership and the impact it would have on global governance. Realism focuses on strategic interests; idealism focuses on moral values. But this "either my interest or my value" approach toward international relations is not compatible with the identity of a global leader. The essence of international relations is "relationship," instead of interests or values. I therefore propose a connectivist perspective, which focuses on full fledged connection through functional instrumentation and relational inclusion. It is my hope that this theoretical construction can provide a sustainable and universally applicable policy orientation to policy makers.

Therefore, in terms of the orientation and contents of this book, it is both theoretical and prescriptive. It attempts to provide a connectivist perspective on international relations, as well as about human society in general. On this theoretical basis, I would like to offer some prescription about world peace and global governance. I have high hopes that the discussions in this book will develop into a new theoretical paradigm to facilitate our common understanding about the global village we share as our home.

With the purpose of constructing a potential paradigm in mind, I strive to focus on originality instead of on comprehensiveness. I believe the strength of the arguments in this book lays less in its comprehensiveness than in its originality. The assumption is that the readers have their own frame of reference when they read the book; they are knowledgeable enough to make their own judgments as long as they read the theory and understand its logical illustration. Therefore, the book avoids detailed factual descriptions unless they are very necessary for logical reasoning.

Scholars and researchers in the field of international studies are most likely to be interested in the theoretical arguments and practical prescriptions in this book. The field has long been dominated by realism and liberalism, the two different ways of thinking that framed the ideas of thousands. This book develops a third way, which is termed connectivism. It focuses on another distinctive form of power but is not power as we know it. It starts from answering a key question in international studies: why do we say, from the "social" perspective, that the world is not anarchic? It therefore proposed two key concepts to understand the global governance system: connective authority and connective democracy. Both of them are socially empowered through connections. Unlike other types of power that need "soft" institutions to legitimize them, the connective power itself develops from, and at the same time brings about, "soft" institutional constructions, as well as strengthening "hard" power in a systematic way. In the mean time, it differs from post-modern understandings of international relations. It does not enshrine "social construction" which means everything is changeable depending on the process of discourse. Connective power through structural functioning and social connections are tangible, accumulative, and objectively measurable. It is more a structural thing, instead of a fluid process. Because of theoretical constructions like connective power and its constructive impact on a new form of global governance system, scholars and researchers of international studies might find value in the connectivist construction of international studies.

Obviously, this book is an ivory tower theoretical construction. But it has very strong policy implications. I believe what the policy makers need is strategic outlines instead of comprehensive tactics. If any theory can provide long term and universally applicable strategic guidance to the policy makers, it will fulfill a great purpose. I am writing this book with this hope in mind. This book has answered some key practical questions in international relations, such as: how is it possible to construct a system of global governance for the purpose of maintaining a peaceful world? How can we make the American leadership constructive and effective in this process? Policy makers in both the government and the corporate world across the globe might be attracted by the theoretical construction and its potential policy significance in this book. Hopefully the connectivist theoretical construction of the global society and its governance can provide some food for thought for them and help them make sense of the world when they deal with their daily routines.

As a scholar who has been doing research in the fields of sociology, history and political science, as well as one who has been interested in philosophy, social psychology and cultural anthropology for more than 20 years, I attempt to use this book to develop heart-to-heart connections with other scholars in these fields. I would hope that, as a theoretical construction on the basis of interdisciplinary inquiry, this book will draw attention from scholars and researchers in the fields of international studies, sociology, political science, history, anthropology and philosophy.

First, the theory of connectivism is a baby of sociology. It is deeply rooted in its major theories. Its fundamental understanding about the global village is based on structural-functionalism, conflict theory, and network theory. At the same time, it has reformulated the structure of sociological theory as a whole. This book might be able to serve sociologists in their endeavor toward the sociological understanding of international relations.

Political scientists in general might also be interested in the concepts in this book, especially the concept of "connective democracy," because it is potentially a genuine alternative to the other two types of democracy as we know them. Political science has devoted much of its energy to exploring representative and participatory democracy for almost the entirety of its existence. The concept of "connective democracy" might bring fresh air to the field and stimulate new thoughts about institutional constructions of the political system domestic and international alike.

Each generation creates its own historical accounts and interprets the past differently according to their contemporary frames of mind. Historians are always actively seeking theoretical ideas during their historical research. Great historians are, at the same time, great social philosophers and profound theorists. I hope that historians will find the connectivist approach interesting and helpful.

This book is also a philosophical book. Philosophers will likely find that this is a book about historical philosophy with sociological flavor. It is a long established tradition in the field of philosophy that the study of the nature of human society is a highly respected academic pursuit. Philosophers in general are both producers and consumers of new social theories. In classic eras from Plato to Kant, in fact, social science was part of philosophy.

Journalists are always sensitive about fresh ideas, by training and by professional necessity. There is a trend in mass media that values new theories and ideas and regards them as equally important as dramatic events and abnormal behaviors. Journalists recognize that ideas shape the world and dramatic actions are constantly dictated by fresh ideas. This book might be one of the many to serve journalists' professional pursuits in discovering new ideas and predicting their potential impact on practical global trends.

Last but not least, a group of people who might be interested in this book are concerned people in the general public. Business people look for theories to guide their decision-making; young students have a burning desire for fresh ideas to feed their intellectual hunger; educators need new frames of thinking to refresh their teaching; and many, many more concerned people across the globe are actively looking for theories to help them make sense of their own lives and the world around them. It is my hope that this book can serve them well.

The ideas of this book originated more than twenty years ago in 1986 when I was doing field research in the area of rural development in Northern China. When I was trying to apply the principles of the modernization theory in the field to help rural people get out of poverty, I discovered that modern technology and external investment stopped working at the point where they were no longer able to facilitate social connections between the local people and the outside helpers. We were there to play a functional role in their lives instead of imposing our "better" way of life onto them. I realized that the most effective way to develop rural economy was not introducing costly and fancy new "things." It would be a waste of time if we focused on those "things." All the good intentions, all the means of modernization, including the artificially introduced new technologies, new educational system, new forms of production and its management system, as well as new ideology and the political system it promoted, would not work unless we genuinely connected to the local people through local elites who, one way or another, had previous experiences in dealing with the outside world. It was the development of the web of social connections that was worth the time and energy. It was the web of social connections that enabled the new "things" to take root and therefore produce amazing results. My colleagues at Shangdong Academy of Social Sciences whom I worked together with for more than five years deserve my deep gratitude. Among them, I would like to especially thank my dear friends Weng Huiming, Yan Hongyuan, Wu Weihua, Li Shanfeng and Zhang Jingjin.

Professor Andrew Walder's book *Communist Neo-Traditionalism* helped me clarify my thoughts further. Although his book has a strong rational choice flavor, it is nonetheless a profound exploration based on network theory. I learned the way to formulate theoretical ideas in the general framework of American sociology. I am very thankful to Professor Walder for being my first mentor in the American academia.

In Spring 1992 at Harvard University when I audited Professor Samuel Huntington's class on the waves of democracy across the globe, I related his idea about democracy to my experience in the field of rural development. I then realized that liberal or representative democracy might not work in the rural area where I worked, not because of the low level economic development, not because of the local people's low level of education, and not because of government's oppression, either. It would be the low level of social connections the liberal/representative democracy could generate that made it hard for this ideology to take root. What the local people needed was the leadership through acceptable power. And the only way to develop acceptable power was through playing a functional role in their lives in the process of developing social connections. We must build up the connection by involving them in the areas that they cared about the most. The key issue is how to empower the local people by enabling them to do the things they cared about the most but did not have the means to make it become reality, instead of power-over them by imposing onto them something they cared little about. Authority through connection was therefore the key concept for a successful rural development project and the Weberian formulation was obviously not adequate. I predicted at that time that the seemingly powerful wave of liberal democracy across the globe was in fact shallow and superficial. It was only an aftermath of the Cold War and would lose its steam as soon as the Cold War dust settled. As genuine believers of democracy, we need to search for its new forms.

Dr. Janet Surrey, a leading scholar in psychology and one of the founding members of the Stone Center at Wellesley College, and Dr. Steve Bergman (Samuel Shem), a novelist and a Harvard Medical School psychiatrist, introduced me to "relational psychology" in 1992 and have continuously provided me with the newest progress in that field. I got many theoretical inspirations from the knowledge they provided me. For that and for much other help I received from them, I am extremely grateful.

This idea was eventually developed into a concept I then termed "relational authority." I presented this concept in Professor Eve Spangler's class at Boston College in Fall 1994 and got an A+. I am so grateful to Professor Spangler for her encouragement and guidance. In the semester that followed, I did an independent study with Professor Paul S. Gray. The term paper for that class is "On Relational Authority." The theoretical construction got a big boost because of Professor Gray's strong interest in this concept—he even helped me formulate some ideas and edit the paper. I am deeply grateful to him for his theoretical guidance and editing efforts.

I then looked for empirical grounding for this new concept. It proved to be unexpectedly difficult. Part of the reason was that the concept "relational authority" was still in a very preliminary stage of development and needed so much work to reformulate. It took me three years to ground my theory of social connectedness (a reformulated and broadened relational authority theory) on Watergate Affair, the historical event that had the potential to empirically illustrate my theory. I used two more years to work on my theory and finish my dissertation on Watergate. In this long process, Professors William Gamson and Diane Vaughan helped me tremendously. As my dissertation committee Chair and member and as leading scholars in the fields of political sociology and organizational studies, they guided me through the whole process with their profound theoretical insights, rich research experiences, and broad knowledge of the American political system and beyond. The idea of permeability of a political system was from Professor Gamson and the theory of interdependence was introduced to me by Professor Vaughan. Their professionalism and kind-hearted enthusiasm supported me through my last few years at Boston College.

I would like to mention another professor who has helped me so much both academically and personally. Professor William Harris was my dearest friend and mentor in the Sociology Department at Boston College. He introduced me to many key concepts and theories that became the building blocks of the connectivist approach, such as the psychological balance theory and sociological social capital theory. His wisdom was the guide that enabled me to go through the difficult process of theory construction without giving up in the middle.

My book, *Understanding Power through Watergate—the Washington Collective Power Dynamics,* was published in 2005. It highlighted the social dynamics in which the formal political institutions were embedded. For example, the concept "Washington collective power dynamics" indicated that, rather than the separation of institutionalized powers, the essence of the system is socially sharing power. The American democratic system worked in the case of Watergate because of its effectiveness in connecting politically powerful people in high circles—it could effectively weed-out the people who abused their power against the norm of social connection. It also pointed out the weakness of the system: the social connection between the politically powerful and the less powerful is weak and superficial.

However, I still feel the theory is not fully presented in my Watergate book. There are many issues which needed to be clarified and many points which needed to be sharpened. I discovered that international studies is a good field for me to further develop my theory of connectivism. It is very fortunate that my article "Transactional Authority and the American Hegemony" was accepted by the First Global Conference for International Studies in Istanbul, Turkey, in August 2005. At the conference, Dr. Miriam Prys of Oxford University, as the discussant of my panel, provided me with many insightful and constructive comments. Her comments elevated my knowledge about the cutting-edge research in the field of international studies onto a higher level.

In writing this book, I am clearly aware of the fact that I am undertaking a huge task, so huge that it is beyond my limited knowledge and wisdom. Fortunately, I have been a recipient of so much kind help throughout the duration of this project. The theoretical research for this book was supported by the STARS grant offered by Westfield State College of Massachusetts. I am deeply grateful to Drs. Bagley, Mangaliso, Kersting and Mildred for their help in the Sociology Department when I applied for this grant and to Dr. Rasool for her support on the college level. Furthermore, the warm collegiality my colleagues created in the department and the leadership Dr. Rasool provided on the college level have greatly facilitated my research and writing. This ambitious project would not have been possible without their sincere support.

I would like to thank Ms. Patti D. Belcher, Acquisition Editor of University Press of America, for her enthusiastic support and professionalism. Ms. Sara Lewis deserves my deepest gratitude for her editing efforts. It is her superb editing skill that has made this book presentable.

I salute all the people who contributed to the advancement of knowledge in the academic fields of sociology, political science (international studies included), history, philosophy, social psychology, and cultural anthropology, such as the giants who already passed away— Max Weber, Karl Marx, Emile Durkheim, Georg Simmel, Talcott Parsons, Lewis Coser, Richard Emerson and Hans J. Morgenthau, and those contemporary giants such as Kenneth N. Waltz, Theda Skocpol, Robert O. Keohane, John J. Mearsheimer, John Ikenberry, Mark Granovetter, Nan Lin, and Robert D. Putnam. It is only because these academic giants offered their shoulders for me to stand on, that I can have the opportunity to try to be taller than I actually am.

I am grateful to my family members for their support and their patience in the process of my writing this book: my mother Ma Xiaoji, my sisters Dr. Dong Huijia and Dr. Dong Yijia, my brothers-in-law, Dr. Liu Chen and Dr. Wang Gongchao, as well as my nieces and nephew, Joy, David, and Jianjian. My cousins Ma Tianzong, Yang Huan, and Hu Hong also deserve my deep gratitude. I owe them countless family obligations because of the time I have spent writing this book and they have been so forgiving of my absent mindedness when I was carried away by my concentration on this book. They are also the warmest and most enthusiastic supporters for this undertaking. Their warmth melted countless icy moments when I was frozen in unsolvable theoretical puzzles.

My wife, Dr. Qin Dongxiao, has been a follower of relational psychology since she began her graduate study in 1992. As an accomplished psychologist, she also contributed the contextual approach, as well as some new concepts, to the advancement of relational psychology. In the mean time, her intellectual discussions with me enhanced my belief in the connective approach and enriched my knowledge in relevant fields. The "endless list" that she has been doing around the house freed me from many household duties and made it possible for me to concentrate on this book. As two "aspects" of one family, we, willingly or unwillingly, share everything, from difficulties to joys, from setbacks to achievements. This nature of oneness is highlighted most saliently between us. We are connected and we are together, "for better and/or for worse."

My son, Daniel Zai, has been the everlasting inspiration to me. It is the burning desire to do something meaningful for a peaceful and happy life for his generation that has been driving me throughout the entire research and writing process. It is the sense of connection as a father to his beloved son that has allowed me to endure through many tormented moments in my life. My profound concern about the future of human society is deeply rooted in my love for my son. I enshrine human connections because I am deeply connected to my son and this connection has transformed me and made me a part of something bigger than myself. If this book can contribute something, large or small, to the endeavor for world peace and human prosperity, it should be attributed to my son who distilled in me the faith in human connections.

D.T.J.
Wilbraham, Massachusetts
November 2007

Chapter One

The Social Order of a Global Village

AN ANARCHIC WORLD?

For the purpose of exploring global governance and leadership, the first theoretical question we have to address is: what is the fundamental nature of the international society? Is it "a society" at all? Most people in the field of international relations use one word to characterize it: anarchy. Since, in an anarchic world, everybody is out for themselves, the realists, defensive and offensive alike, would focus on balance of power and distribution of capabilities.[1]

Liberal institutionalists would emphasize both international and domestic institutions and hope they can more or less regulate and order the anarchy; social constructionists talk about the power of states as agencies by asserting "Anarchy is what states make of it!" But the fundamental argument is, as Robert Keohane summarizes:

> Two elements of international structure are constants: (1) the international system is anarchic rather than hierarchic, and (2) it is characterized by interaction among units with similar functions. The third elements of the structure, the distribution of capabilities across the states in the system, varies from system to system, and over time.[2]

It is true that politically and economically, the world is anarchic. Politically, the fact is that there is no world government. Since there is no government to propose and enforce laws, individual actors' political behavior would be very likely oriented towards power politics. As Mearsheimer points out:

> This cycle of violence will continue far into the new millennium. Hopes for peace will probably not be realized, because the great powers that shape the international

system fear each other and compete for power as a result. Indeed, their ultimate aim is to gain a position of dominant power over others, because having dominant power is the best means to ensure one's own survival. Strength ensures safety, and the greatest strength is the greatest insurance of safety. This is a tragic situation, but there is no escaping it unless the states that make up the system agree to form a world government. Such a vast transformation is hardly a realistic prospect, however, so conflict and war are bound to continue as large and enduring features of world politics.[3]

Economically, beyond the power of market—the naked demand and supply relationship— it is the power of each individual nation-state that dominates trade and capital flow. It is obvious that anarchy does not mean chaos. We see order in the international interactions. But the order is not based on established institutions; rather, it is a reflection of the power relationships among the nations and defined by the "great powers." As Kenneth Waltz asserts: international structures "are defined not by all of the actors that flourish within them but by the major ones."[4]

All of this highlights the strength of the Westphalian sovereign nation-state system. The most fundamental unit of action in international relations has been and will be the nation-state. A logical conclusion derived from this understanding would naturally be: the drive for power is eternal and the result is the ever-lasting escalated power struggle among the nations. Since all international institutional constructions are too weak to be fully functional, the balance of power offers the temporary solution for human beings to live together. And the only hope for a long-term peaceful co-existence is based on domestic institutions. Liberal democracy is therefore enshrined as the only effective vehicle that can save the human beings from killing and destroying each other. If the balance of power cannot carry us for long and democratic peace is proven not so effective after all, we would have to be desperately pessimistic about our own future. It is at this point we see the limitation of political and economic understanding about the nature of international relations.

However, socially, we might be able to see a different world through a different lens.

First of all, we have to define what is "social." Max Weber provided a classic definition: "Action is social in so far as, by virtue of the subjective meaning attached to it by the acting individual (or individuals), it takes account of the behavior of others and is thereby oriented in its course."[5] According to this classic definition, we might say that when we are together with others, we have to take these others into account when we act. The reason we take others into account is that our relationship with them is meaningful to us, negatively or positively. Otherwise, anything "social" would not be possible. In this case, we must focus on our relationships with others when we look after our individual interests. As Blumer stressed, social action is a fitting together of individual actions: "Each individual aligns his action to others by ascertaining what they are doing or what they intend to do—by getting the meaning of their acts."[6] Therefore, the very meaning of social is that togetherness makes individuals feel the meaning of their relationships with others and act upon their connections with them.

There is no doubt that international society is also a social world. We are together anyway, everybody included, whether we like it or not. The key issue is: how free are we? We are born into relationships and we have to live in and through them. In terms of relationships, we usually do not have much choice. We have to accept what we have—we not only have to face the impossibility of choosing parents and family and the difficulty of choosing community and country, but also have to deal with the impossibility of leaving this planet. As Durkheim mentioned: "Men cannot live together without acknowledging, and consequently, making mutual sacrifices, without tying themselves to one another with strong, durable bonds."[7]

The notion of relational connection is not only meaningful between or among each person, but also meaningful to each nation-state. They therefore have to take others into consideration when they act. We live in a 192 household global village which has become a tightly knit social unit. Each household is bound tightly by the very fact we have to live together and deal with each other. And, especially when we deal with each other, we have to be inclusive to include as many "household" as possible. There is no escaping unless we are determined to fail. The social connection and togetherness are inescapable!

However, many theoretical arguments in the field of international relations are based on an individualistic notion. They assume that we can selectively detach ourselves from the people we do not like and intentionally attach ourselves to anyone we do like. We therefore have freedom of choice in the world—we can freely pursue our self-defined self-interests and insist on our moral values. So war of all against all is inevitable unless there is a world government, or some other institutions for that matter, to regulate our behaviors. But, in fact, this individualistic notion is a costly luxury and an unrealistic illusion.

In this global village, the fact is that others exist and try to engage with us. This fact itself is a powerful relational force we have to deal with. The essence here is that while we are dealing with others' interests or values, we are in fact dealing with the very relationship between them and us. The conventional theories, realism and idealism alike, leave too much freedom for us to choose whether we want to engage in the relationships or not. But in fact, we do not have much freedom. We are not free from each other; we cannot freely pursue our self-interests without tying ourselves to others with inescapable social bonds—we do not have a choice but to take others into account when we act. Once we have to take others into account for every action we undertake, they are part of us and we are part of them. Internally or domestically, we are shaped by them and they are shaped by us when all of us construct our understanding of self-interest; externally or internationally, relationship becomes paramount—whatever self-interests we pursue, we have to pursue it in the frame of certain types of relationships.

The inevitable and inescapable exchange is a good example to highlight the powerful force that holds nations together and makes them form a global community. As Simmel pointed out, "All external and internal motives that bind individuals together may be examined with respect to their implementation of the exchange which not only holds society together once it is formed but, in large measure, forms it."[8] As he notes, Simmel's words are by no means limited to the simple and immediate exchange of good and products. When we exchange with others, we are engaging in a relationship. We naturally subjectify the relationship by attaching meanings to the exchange. We experience each other and develop feelings. In a subtle way, we form a bond, which can be positive or negative. But we have to take each other into consideration when we act. Therefore, this bond becomes a force that molds each of us into a proper role in the relationship.

International relations are full of cooperation. It is not because we are good people so we cooperate. We cooperate because of necessity in a tightly knit web of international ties. It is not only when we face some common threat like large scale pandemic that we spontaneously cooperate. Our cooperation is also based on the sense of togetherness which is deeply rooted in closed ties formed among us. Cooperation emerges through faith, tradition, routinized ways of life, and custom. As rational beings, we are not automatically focus on single-minded pursuit of our self-defined interests. On the contrary, we, as rational beings, rationalize our cooperation with others in countless ways through contracts and organizational constructions. Through contract, we form interdependency; through organizational constructions, we make others instruments of the organization while we become instruments, too. We therefore develop utilitarian ties, which is revealed through the sense of togetherness. Most of the time, it is not because we want to cooperate, it is because we have to.

As the case of cooperation, coercion is also omnipresent in international relations. Coercion here is a mode of social interaction rather than interest deprivation or value imposition. Although it rests ultimately on force, it is relational in nature. Coercion may be imposed by force in its physical sense; it can also be accomplished through ridicule of the world's public opinions, ostracism from the world community, denial of protection, and the withholding of recognition.

In international relations, coercion has functional importance. It makes the nations behave the way they ought to. Even the most powerful nations are subject to some forms of this type of coercion. They have to follow the conventions of international norms; they have to obey the fundamental humanitarian rules the world community has developed throughout its history. As Simmel points out: "Occasionally the consciousness of being under coercion, of being subject to a superordinate authority, is revolting or oppressive — whether the authority be an ideal or a social law, an arbitrarily decreeing personality or the executor of higher norms. But for the majority of men, coercion is probably an irreplaceable support and cohesion of the inner and outer life."[9]

Global village, therefore, is not an empty phrase without power and substance. The very fact that we are together no matter what is itself powerful enough to shape our fundamental understanding about international relations. To understand international relations simply from the political and economical perspective is far from enough. We must bring the "social" back in.

There are at least two practical issues that might emerge if we look at the world from the social perspective. First, since the social world is inescapable and it is inevitable for us to be together, we share vulnerability. The common notion of shared vulnerability regards it as something from mother nature — the eruption of a pandemic, global warming, etc. I would add that shared vulnerability is also about the high possibility that we may hurt each other to the extent that we die together, or at least live miserable lives together. The source of it comes from the very fact of togetherness. If one part of the world lives miserably, the other parts would also feel the consequences of that misery. We cannot afford to pursue our own interests without taking others into consideration. The "everybody is out for themselves" image of anarchy is an unrealistic illusion. The reason is simple: the people living in misery would, sooner or later, forcefully bother the people who were not miserable. We have a high possibility of hurting each other if we are not able to keep relationships between or among us. The logic of conventional warfare is: "I kill you so I'll live a better life." However, in a tightly knit global village, the logic of warfare might be: "I kill myself so you'll either die with me or live a costly and fearful life." Compared to the latter, the former becomes easy to understand and easy to deal with whereas the latter, the core logic of terrorism, would effectively drag everybody into a miserable life.

Another practical issue from the social perspective is about inclusiveness. We face a situation in which we have to deal with a partner who is 51% friend and 49% enemy or to deal with a rival who is 51% enemy and 49% friend. Since we are together and we share so much, we have to include everyone and, as a consequence, be able to endure constant tensions with virtually everybody on the one hand, and to limit conflict to a certain level on the other.

It is highly dialectic that we have to constantly fight for our interests but we also have to make sure we do not hurt others too much.

It is also a misunderstanding that the nation-states play similar functions in the global system. In fact, in this tightly knit global village, different nations play different roles: some play a key role in facilitating the adjustment of human society as a whole to nature and therefore allow participants to make a better living; some contribute more in maintaining the common security and social control; some of them are more socially connected and therefore support a more productive process of integration among nations; some are more active and effective in terms of shaping the direction of human society as a whole. If we regard the common goals of human society as a whole as peaceful co-existence and living a better life, some of the nation-states clearly play more important functions than others.

Power and capability cannot be regarded as individually rooted and therefore separated from functional role-playing and relational connection. A nation-state's strength and wealth, to a large extent, depends on its structural position in the international system and the functional role it plays. We usually attribute the source and origin of national strength and wealth to domestic factors, like economic structure, political system, and culture. But the fact is that it is impossible to separate the domestic factors from international ones. In fact, all the domestic factors work in the context of international relations and the latter shape the former before they are effective in reality.

In sum, if we use a Buddhist language here, we might say: we are holding each other hostage! This notion might be too dramatic, but it is somewhat true. We know that gated communities are very expensive; only the very rich can afford to live in them. But it is very unfortunate that many thinkers in the field of international relations think about exactly same idea of developing a "gated nation." When they propose ideas to deal with the situation of a global village, they suggest expensive security measures: hire more people in military and other areas of national security, increase control of the borders, invent and apply more sophisticated equipment, etc. The whole idea is separatedness—be strong, be individually strong, don't be together with others, don't be inclusive, deal with friends only and kill all the enemies and at the same time stay away from the rest of the people as much as possible. Even if—and it is a very big "if"—we can afford spending, spending and spending on building a "gated nation," and we are powerful enough to be able to separate ourselves from others, are we going to be happy living within the walls? What's the meaning of living a miserable life filled with fear and being combative all the time while seeking enemies to kill? Aren't we worried that we are going to lose friends and partners while living an isolated and segregated life simply because of fear or for the purpose of killing our enemies?

Fortunately, international relations do not work that way. International relations as an aspect of social life cannot be characterized as anarchy; they are not war of all against all. When nation-states are out to pursue their self-interests, they most likely put relationships before those interests and pursue them in the framework of the relationships. From the social perspective, international relations can be characterized with one phrase: functional and relational connection. It is true that individual human beings are smart, but not so reliable. But human social relationships are not necessarily corrupt. The fundamental cognitive base regarding international relations as anarchy is the worship of government—a typical Hobbesian notion. The basic assumption is that without a government human beings cannot keep a constructive social relationship—they are bound to be out killing each other. But I enshrine human relational connections and believe they are the genuine source of power that determines the daily activities of human society in a orderly way.

CLASH OF CIVILIZATIONS?

Since the publication of Samuel Huntington's book *Clash of Civilizations*, Civilization has become a hot topic for us to understand the driving forces behind the dynamics of international relations. According to Huntington and some others, civilization generally means the overall way of life of a people. "It involves values, norms, institutions, and modes of thinking to which successive generations in a given society have attached primary importance." "It is a space, a cultural area in which a collection of cultural characteristics takes roots and historical whole manifested itself." "Religion is the ideological core of a civilization." "The collection of special organizational forms is the carriers of a civilization."[10]

Huntington's "clash of civilizations" thesis can be summarized as the following:

a. The post-Cold War world is a world of eight major civilizations: Western, Latin American, African, Islamic, Confucian, Hindu, Orthodox, Japanese. The most important countries in the world come overwhelmingly from different civilizations. The key issue on the international agenda involves differences among civilizations.
b. Cultural commonalities and differences, cultural identities, shape the interests, antagonism, and associations of states. The local conflicts most likely to escalate into broader wars are those between groups and states from different civilizations. The predominant patterns of political and economic development differ from civilization to civilization.

c. Power is shifting from the long predominant West to non-West civilizations. Global politics has become multipolar and multicivilizational. A civ-
ilization-based world order is emerging: societies sharing cultural affini-
ties cooperate with each other; efforts to shift societies from one
civilization to another are unsuccessful. And countries group themselves
around the lead or core states of their civilization.[11]

The theme of social connectivism shares with the thesis of "clash of civilizations" about the limits of the social connections of nation-states. The reason is clear: culture facilitates social connections. The power of social connections might hit its limit along civilizational lines from time to time. But
the theory of social connectivism asserts that, fundamentally, social connections have the potential power to drive for a cultural/civilizaitonal conver-
gence. It therefore differs from the "clash of civilizations" argument in the
following three aspects:

First, the struggle for expanding social connections might be the genuine
content of the clash of civilizations. Because social connections are tangible,
they are more closely related to material and strategic interests. It has the direct impact on the effective social interactions and structural functions that
determine the order and dynamics in global affairs. The theory of social connections emphasizes two aspects of culture— the material side and the spiritual one, whereas the clash of civilizations theory virtually overlooks material culture and regards religion as the core of civilizations.

Second, social connections are more about contemporary power dynamics
and less about historical cultural accumulations. While it pays attention to the
chain effect of historical accumulation and takes into consideration the historical contingency, it places more emphasis on contemporary actions, vi-
sions, and strategies that facilitate immediate and direct social connectedness.

Third, civilizations are about different human groups as distinctive wholes.
The research of civilizations focuses on their distinctiveness. The argument
of social connectivism discusses the universality of social connections and
the struggles both within and between civilizations. It assumes that social
connections are constantly changing and that boundaries are much less stable
and permanent than civilizational lines. Conflicts within civilizations are potentially as significant as the clashes between civilizations.

The theory of social connectivism would further highlight the true dynamic
underneath "clash of civilizations." This dynamic is social in nature and has
three major components. First is that the driving force in each civilization is
nation-states. It is the nation-states within or between civilizations that dictate
the creation and maintenance of the overall way of life through a series of institutional constructions. Since most of these institutional constructions are

oriented toward universal acceptance, they therefore reshape the major characteristics of each civilization. Conflicts over religious issues are largely reflections of the web of international connections among nation-states.

Second, in the process of domination and manipulation of religious or civilizational symbols, the dominant elites in each nation-state marginalize a proportion, large or small, of the general population by failing to connect to them or by intentionally insulating them. The degree of social connections between the dominant groups and the general public in each nation-state is the essence of power dynamics within or across civilizations.

Third, the "clash of civilizations" thesis overlooks the functional aspect of the civilizational structure as a whole. One civilization may be more functional in terms of providing a spiritual foundation to facilitate a universalized legal system while the other may be spiritually stronger in promoting interpersonal, inter-group, or international ties. Civilizations have their unique and different strengths and weaknesses. They, therefore, may play different roles in enriching the overall structural strength of human society as a whole. To clarify each civilization's organizational effectiveness and competitive strength is the essence of social connectivism. It regards the level of functional connection to other civilizations as the strength of each civilization. Some civilizations might be socially more functional, more oriented toward connections, and therefore more organizationally effective than other civilizations. In the long and ever-lasting human history, the clash of civilizations is a dynamic that formulates a stronger, more adaptive, and more productive way of life of human society as a whole.

THE CONVERGENCE OF SOCIAL FORCES IN POLITICAL, ECONOMIC AND CULTURAL SPHERES

The Socially Connected Nation-States as Global Villagers

The first force we need to examine is nation-states. As we commonly understand, a nation is a group of people who are tied to each other by a common past, a common language, a similar way of life, and similar pursuit of interests based on common experience. These characteristics distinguish them from other peoples. When such a nation organizes itself also into a political entity, its political structure is materialized by its legislative function to set up rules for the nation to follow and its enforcement function to make sure everybody follows the rules. A nation-state therefore takes shape and it has the legitimated power to monopolize the use of force within its borders.

A nation-State is also a special kind of economic organization. It is in a strong position to interfere effectively with the flow of factors of production (labor, capital, etc.). Its institutional construction regulates the economic activities within its borders and facilitate, or hinder for that matter, the economic drives of its members.

A nation-State is a cultural carrier, too. All the states declare certain ideology as the dominant doctrine as the guiding principles of their policy and legal construction.

However, all these important political, economic and cultural functions of a nation-state would not be possible without independence and self-determination. The most elementary function of a nation-state is the defense of the life of its citizens and the nation's free existence from other nation-states. This task is represented and accomplished by the leading elite group of the nation at each specific historical moments. Whenever this leading group is no longer able to accomplish the task, it must yield, either through peaceful transformation or violent destruction, to an internal force or an external one that is capable of that defense. A nation-state's "sovereignty" is the claim to the right to do whatever it can to defend itself and its citizens. The drive behind the dynamics of national sovereignty is similar to individual's motivation to maintain what they have and minimize loss. This is a highly social task—power derived from internal strength is only relevant when it can pass the test in international contests. Internal strength only works through international society.

In the mean time, nation-states are also looking for maximizing their gain. Not only the strong make efforts to increase their control and possession and strengthen their power through conquest, through building and shaping up international institutions and through functioning well and connecting widely, the weak are also aspired to do so. It is hard to say Canada is stronger than the US based on the conventional understanding. However, Canada can often maximize its gain while the US cannot. National identity, therefore, is not what a culture heritage it has, nor its military or economic power. "Soft" power and "hard" power only matter when they are multiplied by the social connective power. National identity hence has less to do with what the nation as an individual has or is; it has more to do with what a position the nation occupies in the global village on specific issues and on common concerns. A nation's identity is defined by its functional position and international connection on specific issues and on global structure as a whole.

The global society has become more and more interconnected. It is undergoing a strong nation-states dominated networking process. One of the cultural agents for the trend of unified way of life is the ever unifying educational system that reshapes people and transforms them from diversified cultural carriers to universal human resource serving the needs of capitalist expansion and nation-state connection. The legal constructions in nation-states across the globe and the emphasis on human rights are two very effective instruments for nation-states to smooth out the political and legal roadblocks in the process of their social connections and achieve at least a unified cognitive framework. Even the rogue nations are required to play by the rules by the majority of the members of the global village. Technologies facilitate the ever-expanding capacity for this globalized cognitive framework to reach every corner of the globe.

Barriers are clearly there in the process. Boundaries between nation-states have shaped people's loyalties in a powerful way; countless diversified groups in nation-states are exerting their power over the construction of national interests and the understanding about national identity; legal systems and business norms are still far from unified— the rules are different in many areas; competitions among nation-states across the globe over how to divide natural resources have strong impact on global politics; civilizational line is still clear—people are still loyal to their culture, their perceptions about their interests in the international relations are still, to a large extent, shaped by their different way of life. All of this would tell us a fact: people are still divided, more than united. But the trend is also clear: the power of social connections across nation-states is the driving force behind the dynamics of creating a "village life" on a global scale.

The Dynamics of Capitalist Expansion

Another major force in current global village is the force of capitalist expansion. Capitalists are the people who own the means of production and pursuit profit with it. They function powerfully through capitalism. Capitalism is an economic system in which the means of production (capital) are privately owned and the profits generated by the means of production are distributed according to the amount of capital people own. It is also a political system in which those who own capital are legally positioned to control those who do not.

The theory of social connectivism emphasizes capitalists' social power instead of their economic power. The global triumph of the entire capitalist institutional construction, from its financial market to it managerial organization through manufacturing and marketing to product consumption, enables a special type of social power, as well as economic power. The essence is that the whole capitalist institution provides a complete institutional setting for social reach to take place. In this capitalist institutional setting, capitalist elites can socially reach a vast population through organizing the essential items of their daily lives in the areas of material production and consumption. As a means of social reach, capitalist institution is viewed more than economic sphere. Pure individualistic rational choice must give way to the social constructions of social relationships. Social connectivism pinpoints "social" factors and mechanisms beyond the economic sphere in capitalist institutional constructions.

The strength of the American system is its strong capitalist institutional constructions. Capitalist institutions, including their financial, marketing, and manufacturing organizations, as well as the legal and educational systems that serve their needs and the political and ideological constructions that support the capitalist establishment, are the few established institutions that are capable of supporting the social reach on a global scale. Although their function is currently regarded as primarily economic, they have the high potential to become more effective vehicles in which to carry the active agency of social reach to its place across the globe.

On the scene of the global village, the contemporary capitalism is dominated by two forms, one is multinational corporation and the other is global corporation (as it is defined by Kenichi Ohmae[12]). Both multinational and global corporations are huge businesses that operate in many nations across the globe. The fundamental difference is that the former do not integrate the local elements of human resource, production, marketing and service forces while the latter fully utilize and integrate the local elements and therefore transform itself completely. The former are still bounded by national borders and the latter are the true business without boundary.

Therefore, the global corporation is the major form of capitalist institution that is capable of both economic and social reach on a global scale. It is different from the old-fashioned multinational corporations in the sense that it integrates the local elements of economic factors, from finance and investment to research and development, from manufacturing and marketing to customer service, into one unified organization across the globe. Unlike multinational corporations which are still bounded by national borders in the organizational form of mother company/baby company, global corporations have fundamentally transformed themselves into borderless institutions. This type of global integration of economic factors has great potential to promote social reach and expand the social sphere of social power. It can be the objective force to push the ever-expanding process of social connection; it can also be the intersubjective force that promotes social connections across the globe through its interactions in the process. Government and corporate leaders who are more sensitive to this process would play a bigger role in the process of global social connections. They are in a better position to gain more social power and, therefore, more political power in global politics. It is certain that with integration, there must be conflict. But conflict would push for further integration.

Here, we see capitalism is no longer an economic term, or to a lesser degree a political term. It is rather a social term. It highlights a powerful force of social integration among nations. Through their managerial and educational capability, the global corporations conquered many parts of the world by transforming many men and women who previously loyal and work for their isolated clans, tribes, and/or nations into corporate citizens whose loyalty and efforts are more or less devoted to the corporations in particular and to the global village in general. Through their connections, the global corporations facilitate meaningful transformations among people in different nations and make them dependable partners in a global village. Through their efforts to survive in nations that are so different from their own, the global corporations play functional roles in facilitating the betterment of the existing social system of their hosting nations and develop countless social networks with them. In this way, they effectively strengthened the global social connections. All of this would reveal a fact: the seemingly economic drive of capitalism is in fact a social force and capitalists are the active agents in this process.

Class Division and the Issue of Poverty

More serious threat of the creation of a "village life" on a global scale is the issue of poverty. Class division and struggle is more fundamental than national divide and cultural clash. The definition of poverty can be sketched as the follows:

> Relative Poverty: the deprivation of access to resources that is vital to upward social mobility; Absolute Poverty: a deprivation of resources that is life threatening.

Both relative and absolute poverty have the power to generate strong bottom-up resistance to existing global leadership and affect the global power dynamics in a very powerful way. The driving force behind the poverty issue can be summarized as:

- World-wide capital expansion have made it certain that only those who are useful and usable to the profit-driven capitalist world system can survive regardless of their nationalities and cultures—the resolute result produced by the logic of interdependence.
- This system is characterized by highly complicated high-tech industry and a very sophisticated structure of modern financial system and modern managerial system.

- The more vulnerable structure of production and lower level of productivity of the people in developing countries have destined them less opportunity to get access to the capitalist world system.
- The limited reach of a universalized educational system which has a function to minimize the divide between system insiders and outsiders. Without the educational opportunity to go through the process of socialization, acculturation, and identity reformulation, the people outside the modern school systems are less likely to become insiders of the global system and more likely to be in poverty.

There are two major theories that specifically discuss the issue of poverty. The first one is modernization theory. Its essential ideas can be summarized as the followings: Each nation-state is regarded as an independent system. Therefore, its internal dynamics is the focus. The theory therefore assumes a compatibility of different sub-systems, e.g., political-legal, cultural-educational, and economic systems. If one of them changes, the others will follow. However, since an equilibrium has formed among its subsystems, the traditional system is highly stable. None of its subsystem will change without an external push. The driving force for modernization, therefore, is new technology and foreign aid; and the obstacle for modernization is the traditional way of life. Only after external forces lift one of the subsystems out of the traditional stage can the system as a whole take-off. Individual freedom and rationality are regarded as the driving forces behind the destruction of traditional way of life and the construction of modern life. The prevailing of both of them is regarded as the end result of modernization.

Clearly, this theory regards the issue of poverty as a problem caused by the traditional society and the way to solve it is to model the existing industrialized society and achieve a modernization. It assumes a natural and automatic acceptance of the Western way of production and consumption by the people in the developing world. The industrialized nations are regarded as the inspiration and future to the people of developing nations. Power, domination and exploitation are invisible in this theory despite, in reality, these are the factors that shape a world system. Modernization in reality is a global process that further removes the obstacles for strong nations' global reach that colonialism was not able to deal with. It aims to smooth out and reshape the world order to fit the need of capitalist expansion and strong nation's domination.

The people of developing nations, of course, feel this reality as they personally and intimately experience this process of "modernization." Therefore, it is no wonder to see the fact that they are enthusiastic toward the Western way of production and consumption, but much less so toward the Western civilization as a whole. Since all the sub-systems are interconnected as the modernization theorists would say, it is no wonder to see a fact that people of developing nations are reluctant to be involved in the cause that is supposed to benefit them.

Another theory is the dependency theory. It also starts with the nation-states and focuses on their power to interfere effectively with the flow of factors of production (labor, capital, etc.) through its policies on taxation, anti-trust, labor movement, etc. Since the process of economic development is virtually the result of capital expansion, the nation-states with capital would become the core states and the nation-states without capital would become the peripheral states—a relationship of dependency is therefore formed. The interstate free flow of capital, labor and profits through direct investments and trade exploits peripheral nations' cheap labor, new market and easy raw materials and hence deprives their capability of self-reliance and independence.

According to this theory, the process of modernization is not a solution to the poverty issue. Instead, it is the cause of it. The nation-states that strive for economic development to solve their poverty problem need to rely on policies that facilitate self-reliance.

The key problem of this theory is that it assumes national governments as the major engine of economic development. Can an indigenous government, democratically elected and dictatorship alike, be the solution to the poverty issue? The answer has to be no. The reason is clear: the cause of poverty is the exclusion from the capitalist economic system. It is impossible to solve the poverty issue without being closely involved in global division of labor, global market system, global financial system and modern managerial system. The close causal relationship between poverty and isolation is obvious: lack of access to generate wealth in the capitalist world system is the cause of poverty. The dilemma therefore is: how can the local people connect to the world capitalist system while minimize the possibility of being exploited by the capitalists?

The connectivist policy proposal can be summarized as the followings:

- A rule: localization does not equal to self-sufficiency. Openness is the only way out of poverty.
- The solution: Localized engine of economic development must drive toward capitalist world system. Efforts must be focused on bridging the access the capitalist economy by generating capital in the capitalist economic system and making the products acceptable to the capitalist production and consumption structure.
- The way: A. The social elite model: the engine of economic development must be organically rooted in local community. Well connected local forces are the true effective driving forces that are capable of generating sufficient

local enthusiasm. B. Localization of the engine of economic development: talented people and sufficient investments are necessary for the purpose of providing necessary push and guidance for the local elites. In the mean time, it is essential to facilitate local connections between these outsiders and local social elites. The vast locally oriented social networks serve as the guarantor of keeping profit from pumping out of the local community.

Here, democracy is practiced through relational connections which enables empowerment of the local people. It is an institution that is embedded in social elites' social connections among different social groups. It is materialized through the social ties between social elite groups and ordinary people. Political or economic power in this system is manifested by social power, i.e., political or economic capital, human or financial capital, are embedded in social capital and only the people who have accumulated sufficient social capital in the process of social networking can be members of the elite social group and gain sufficient political power and financial capital in the process.

THE THREE LOGICS OF SOCIAL REACH

The connective theory attempts to go beyond existing theories by seeing the world through the lens of interconnected units of action. The units can be social groups, nation-states, or civilizations. It answers two fundamental questions: What does the connectivist theory assume to be the basic social structure of modern society? How is this social structure assumed to operate?

The concept "social reach" is used here to grasp the genuine driving force of global political order and dynamics. It regards the essence of international relations as distinctive nation-states' capabilities of reaching different nation-states, social groups or people, and thus gain social power this way. Social spheres are therefore formed. They are regarded as the genuine unit of action in global political interactions, whereas the nation-state is regarded as the most important social sphere, in which national elite groups effectively exercise their social connectedness. However, at this moment in the 21st century, the original meaning of social spheres, in which different elite groups of people exercise their social power to socially connect and control as many people and social groups as possible regardless of any institutionalized borders, national borders included, reflects the essence of international, or more accurately, global order and dynamics. Here, power is still a central issue. But it is embedded in the process of social reach.

Social reach, which generates social power and thus creates and maintains social sphere, is embedded in many different types of institutionalized activities. Military conquests, political simulations, business connections and political and economic organizations are all the institutional constructions that facilitate or enable elites to socially reach into different social groups. The power of capitalist enterprises as an effective means to facilitate social reach on a global scale is clearly manifested.

This book aspires to present a new theory termed social connectivism. This theory focuses on the three logics of social reach in international relations and can be summarized as the following:

The power dynamics of international relations are driven by the three logics of international expansion, i.e.: the logic of conquest, the logic of interdependence, and the logic of togetherness. National identity and global governance are therefore shaped by the social connections between nation-states through these three logics.

These three logics work simultaneously in international society. The first logic is the logic of conquest. It highlights the fact that the strong nation-states, for the purpose of expanding their self-constructed national interests, are always seizing opportunities to control and manage the resources (human, natural and social) of the weak nation-states. Under the logic of conquest, the means for the strong nation-states to accomplish their goals of control is to reach through economic expansion and managerial construction, with the military force as the guarantor. It sounds negative when we mention the term "conquest" and it is indeed negative in most cases. But if a conquest can truly play a part in the overall structure of a collective effort instead of imposing the conqueror's will on everything, a conquest might have the potential to bring fundamental change to a corrupted system. For instance, a conqueror might provide the much needed force of security that would enable others to go about doing what they are supposed to without fear and violent disturbance. In this case, conquest is empowering instead of depriving.

The second logic is the logic of interdependence. It reflects two facts. The first is the equal exchange based on international division of labor; the second is that the strong nation-states initiate exchange relationships with the weak ones for the purpose of using their advantageous financial, trading, and productive positions to exploit those that are desperately in need of investment, technology and high-end products. But either way, the key of the logic of interdependence is to be selective about the exchange partners—these partners must be dependable in terms of facilitating an interdependent relationship. The end result of this logic is two folds. It can be inclusive in terms of connecting the people who are regarded as dependable or potentially dependable and forming a connective system. On the other hand, it can be exclusive and alienating to the nation-states, or some social groups inside them, that are not regarded as dependable.

The third logic that also works in the international society is the logic of to-getherness. We are together anyway, whether we like it or not. Everybody lives on this small planet, without alternative in the foreseeable future. The logic produces two driving forces behind the dynamics of global affairs. The first force is the bottom-up force—the people who are oppressed by the logic of conquest and the people who are alienated by the logic of interdependence are the driving force behind the dynamics of global connections. Under the current international system, they are less likely to get organized on a large scale. Very few nation-states would be willing to support these people because of the dominance of the international system by the US and some other strong states. And most other nation-states are the benefactors of the contemporary system. This power structure forces a small proportion of these rebellious groups of people go to the extreme. They are in a situation in which fundamentally they have nothing more to lose. Therefore they are more likely to take an "I die so I can make you live miserably" mentality. What they launch would not be the conventional warfare in which we see a clear boundary of fighting and a clear measure about winning. The only moments that draw public attention are when we are losing. The most effective tactics for these people are terrorist attacks. And since the advancement of technology, they do not need many people to launch large scale operations. A small die-hard elite of these groups have the capability to cause sufficient damage to the international system in general and to some specific nation in particular, especially if they get the weapons of mass destruction in their hands. This type of bottom-up force makes the logic of togetherness clear for everybody in this global village.

Another type of bottom-up force is less visible but more significant. It is the force of unorganized system outsiders who are peaceful but alienated. Poverty and lack of educational opportunities are the surface manifestations. The fundamental issue is the limitation in terms of connective capability of the existing system. It is vital for these people to get effectively connected to the system insiders and to be genuinely included in the operation of the system. Without connection and inclusion, the logic of togetherness would powerfully push more and more system outsiders to struggle, jointly or separately, against the system insiders. This struggle is a powerful bottom-up dynamic with the potential to change the contemporary international system.

The second force is the top-down force generated by the drive of the strong nation-states to maintain their dominant positions and to expand their control over the global system. Because of this drive, they want to reach as many spheres as possible. The nature of exchange on the system level—exchange between the powerful and the powerless, the capitalist and the workers—is unbalanced. For the nation-states or social groups that enter an exchange relationship based on their advantageous positions in the system, the major driving force behind their action is the need to keep the system as it is in order to keep their advantage. It is through the current social system (a set of international relationships) the nation-states or social groups higher in social positions keep their advantageous positions. In order to do so, relationships become paramount. The maintenance and promotion of persistent relationships are the key issues for the dominant nation-states or social groups to minimize the forces that might promote change to the existing system.

However, the other two above mentioned logics limit their options. The economic, managerial and military forces can only control so much and they always risk backfiring. Constructing a relationship of interdependence is not easy—it requires an international system to establish and enforce the rules and a sufficient level of internal development of each partner to reach the standard of dependability. Therefore, the best choice for them is to fully use the logic of togetherness to build up connections. There are two avenues they usually travel. The first is what I termed "authority of instrumentation": to occupy the most functional position in the global system and play the functional roles for the system as a whole and for the other nation-states as parts of the global whole. In this way, they can use other nation-states' resources as their own by manipulating the global system. The second is what I termed "authority of inclusion": to position themselves in the central location of the web of international ties in order to connect as many nation-states as possible and include as many of them as possible in the endeavors the strong nation-states are pursuing. In this way, they can enlist as much help as possible from the nation-states they have no way of controlling directly. We will discuss these two types of authority in detail in Chapter 3.

The logic of togetherness can also serve as the basic criterion by which to measure the strength of power of different nation-states. The more significant a structural function a nation-state can play, the more powerful it is; the more relational its position is in the webs of international ties, the more powerful it is; the more intense a struggle it experienced in the process of its international connections, the deeper its social roots and the more powerful it is; the more the people who play other types of functional roles in society, like the economic elites, technical experts, or political elites, etc., it connects, the more powerful it is; the larger the elite group and the more other socially connected people they can connect, the more powerful it is. We can therefore develop a continuous ratio level measurement based on these criteria about the strength of individual nation-states.

In this way, we can go beyond the "soft power" vs. "hard power" debate. The logic of togetherness highlights a distinctive connective/social power. It is not cultural, not military, not economical and not political. Instead of institutional or cultural power, as is insisted by the soft power assertion, social power is much more tangible and "hard." It is based on clear-cut social relations in a web of international networks. Instead of military or economic power or political power, which are the foci of "hard" power, social power is more fundamental. All the military, economic, and political powers are embedded in certain social relationships and only work as resources, while social relations are the dynamic part of the global power struggle.

The true driving force behind the dynamics of global order is therefore neither anarchic nor hierarchical. It is, rather, a functional network with nation-states' struggle to expand the boundaries of their social reach as its basic characteristic. In the process of struggling for broader and more effective social reach, both anarchic power struggle and hierarchical institutional construction are instruments for the different nation-states to use. But they are far from the whole picture. Social reach is far beyond international institutions and anarchic power struggle. Material resources are regarded as "resources only" waiting to be mobilized by the power of social reach. Whoever consciously or unconsciously uses social power to effectively connect more nation-states globally will likely be the winner of the global struggle under the logic of togetherness.

Although many nation-states have been doing this repeatedly in history and hence have become successful global leaders, few people in the academia and policy think tanks consciously realized the powerful effect of the logic of togetherness in international relations. We talk so much about globalization and regard it as trading and investment, as developing a relationship of interdependence, as an on-going process in the making. But in fact, we have long accomplished globalization. We have been globalized already. We have lived in this global village for a while and we therefore have to deal with each other, no matter whether we like it or not. We hold each other hostage because we can inflict enormous pains on each other—to an extent that we might die together if we cannot live peacefully together. The freedom of selective detachment from people we do not like and intentional involvement with people we like has become an unrealistic luxury. Policies on international relations, therefore, would have to be based on all three logics, especially the logic of togetherness, in order to reflect that reality.

NOTES

1. For the classic view, see Hans J. Morgenthau, *Politics Among Nations*, seventh edition, (Boston: McGraw Hill, 2006); This idea is further developed in Kenneth N. Waltz, *Man, the State, and War: A Theoretical Analysis* (New York: Columbia University Press, 1959); and Kenneth N. Waltz, *Theory of International Politics*, (Read-

ing, MA: Addison-Wesley, 1979). Alos, see Robert Jervis, "Cooperation under the Security Dilemma," *World Politics*, Vol. 30, No. 2, (January 1978):167–214.

2. Robert O. Keohane, *Neorealism and Its Critics*, ed. (New York: Columbia University Press, 1986), 166.

3. John Mearsheimer, *The Tragedy of Great Power Politics,* (New York: W.W. Norton, 2001), xi–xii.

4. Waltz, 1979, 93.

5. Max Weber, *The Theory of Social and Economic Organizations*, trans. by A.M. Henderson and Talcott Parsons (New York: Oxford University Press, 1947), 88.

6. Herbert Blumer, "Society as Symbolic Interaction," in Arnold Rose (ed.), *Human Behavior and Social Processes*, (New York: Houghton Mifflin, 1962), 179–192.

7. Georg Simmel, 1950, "Faithfulness and Gratitude," in Kurt Wolff, ed. and trans., *The Sociology of Georg Simmel,* (New York: Free Press, 1950), 389.

8. Emile Durkheim, 1964, *The Division of Labor in Society*, trans. G. Simpson, (New York: Free Press, 1964), 228.

9. Simmel, 299.

10. Samuel Huntington, *The Clash of Civilizations and the Remaking of World Order* (New York: A Touchstone Book, 1996), 41–44.

11. Huntington, 20–21.

12. Kenichi Ohmae, *Borderless World: power and strategy in the interlinked economy,* (revised edition, New York: HarperBusiness, 1999).

Chapter Two

The Connective Power Dynamics

A WORLD OF STRUCTURAL-FUNCTIONAL CONNECTION

When we are examining the world, we see it as a society. But what exactly is the global society? What are the possible sociological interpretations of it? Both major theories of international studies, realism and idealism alike, have been seeing the world through the lens of individualistic utilitarianism. In my view, the most significant contribution of sociology to the understanding of global society is its conceptualization of "functional togetherness" and "relational connectiveness." It therefore helps us go beyond the individualistic utilitarianism.

Classical economic utilitarianism has been dominating the way people understand society for more than two centuries since Adam Smith published his *An Inquiry into the Nature and Causes of the Wealth of Nations* in 1776. In this theory, humans are viewed as rational individuals who try to maximize their tangible, as well as intangible, gains and, in the mean time, minimize their losses. Social life is like a marketplace where people compete to pursue their rational interests while avoiding being taken advantage of. The pursuit of self-interests is seen as the major driving force in on-going social life.[1]

There are three basic assumptions that support this logic of thinking. First is that the unit of action is individuals. They act individually instead of connectively. There is no interconnected mechanism that shapes individual's perceptions and actions. Second, individuals are rational and fully capable of rational reasoning about what they want and how to get it. They know their "utilities" and therefore have the capability to pursue them. Third, these individuals are free to make choice in the market place and the market as an "invisible hand of order" would therefore work as the driving force to channel the individual rational pursuit in a collective situation. There is no power other than market competition that dictates individual action. Social order is therefore automatically forthcoming as the "invisible hand" works its way out through free competition.

Structural-functionalism questions the three above assumptions. It attempts to provide different answers the questions originally posted by Adam Smith: why and how is society possible? What force holds the social fabric together? Instead of regarding rational individuals as the basic unit of analysis and treating market as the mechanism that holds society together, structural-functionalism sees the social factor that makes society as a whole with individuals as parts of it. Structural-functionalism therefore sees the world through the lens of unity. Its major contribution to social thought in general is its societalist perspective and it therefore provides us with an alternative to classical economic ideas.

First of all, there is a social structure existing prior to any individual's existence. Before each individual comes to this world, there are social relationships and a social order. Individuals are born into this social structure without free choice. We are relational since the moment we come to this world.

Second, this pre-existing social structure plays a powerful role in shaping individuals' wants, needs, and action. Even the most basic human needs such as the need for food are shaped by the social structure—what to eat, how to eat, when to eat, how much to eat, etc. Basic individual needs are more or less predetermined by the society.

Third, the pre-existing social structure makes it very clear to individuals that the only way to get what they want and need is to play the roles prescribed by the socially determined scripts. Role playing therefore transforms individuals from "free agents" into agents of the social structure.

Four, the structure is hierarchical instead of equal. Social power is manifested by social status and works powerfully through exchanges among individuals. Market is a mechanism that connects individuals. But it works under a precondition of unequal social status. Market competition is in fact a "visible hand." The "invisible hand" behind the dynamics of market competition is social power that holds society together.

Emile Durkheim is the person who established structural-functionalism as a school in sociology. He maintains that something "social" is an independent phenomenon; therefore, society is to be viewed as an entity in itself that is not reducible to its parts. In this way, he effectively isolates society as an independent field of study and gives analytical priority to its "whole." Each part is viewed as fulfilling the functions (needs) of the whole. Those that do not fulfill functional needs are abnormal, or even, pathological. He makes it clear that functional analysis focuses on the end or purpose of the parts that serve the needs of the whole. He insists that one of the basic societal needs is integration and the societal functions, especially division of labor, develops to meet this need. All the functional parts complement each other in serving the needs of the whole.[2]

After Durkheim, Talcott Parsons is the person who contributed the most to the structural functional school. His point of departure is, as he states: "The structure of social systems cannot be derived directly from the actor-situation frame of reference. It requires functional analysis of the complications introduced by the interaction of a plurality of actors."[3] In his book *Social System*,[4] he pointed out the complicated needs a system must fulfill if it survives. A key conceptualization is his attempt to discover the mechanism of the systemic connectedness of the system—the integrative force that make the system as a whole possible. He found it and it is, in his term, "institutionalization." It highlights a stable establishment of certain patterns of interaction among individual actors. It infuses cultural values and norms, which, in turn, can become internalized and therefore transform individual actors into functional parts of the whole. The process of institutionalization is the process of system formation and maintenance. Roles are played, rules are formed, patterns of interaction are stabilized, values and norms are set and eventually internalized, and in the end, the social system comes into being.

The system persists through its tendency of equilibration. It is served by two mechanisms that integrate individual actors into the system. The first is socialization, which internalizes norms and values into actors and make them role players and status adherents in the system; the second is social control, which sets up rules and enforces them.

Parsons later further conceptualizes the needs of system existence into four survival requisites: adaptation (to the environment in order to gain sufficient survival capabilities), goal attainment (the ability to prioritize goals and to mobilize resources to accomplish them), integration (the ability to coordinate and sustain viable relationships among individual units), and latency (social control, pattern maintenance and tension management).[5]

When we talk about a social system, we focus easily on the normative side of it. However, there is a more fundamental side of social connection beyond the Durkheimian "mechanical solidarity." Another notion raised by structural-functionalism is division of labors. It is clear that any social whole would not be possible without proper division of labor. The social system which grows from it is termed "organic solidarity." We are socially connected because we choose to be, based on our moral or normative principles; we are also socially connected because we have to be, without choice. This is the notion of structural functioning; because of it, each part of the whole has to strive for connection to the other parts for the purpose of connecting to the whole.

Clearly, current world is not a complete structure. Its parts do not play their roles and functions according to the scripts the structure prescribes. Structural-functionalism therefore is not fully applicable to international studies. For example, to a certain degree, structural-functionalism is a sociological manifestation of idealism in international studies. It enshrines institutionalized "liberal" ideals like freedom, democratic election and vote, equal opportunities, etc. However, it can only add a sociological tone by emphasizing "social functions" in the structure of institutional constructions. If we go beyond pure political structural analysis and think about the social functions of contemporary democratic institutions, we will see that they are only socially functional within national borders. They serve the social function of connecting different social groups of people within a nation. They are less functional in terms of socially connecting groups of people beyond the reach of the political construction.

Structural-functionalism helps us to know that if the system survives, it must have all the elements Parsons has highlighted. A global society is only possible when it somehow develops all these elements. However, structural-functionalism cannot tell us clearly about what is the specific force that shapes this structure and through what dynamics it accomplishes this goal. It never clearly delineates a causal relationship between the survival elements of the social system and their origin. In reality, how can we discern the force that is consciously or unconsciously working on the formation of a social system? To answer this question, the conflict theory in sociology is a useful tool.

A WORLD OF FUNCTIONAL CONFLICT AND DYNAMIC CONNECTION

If we regard the major contribution of structural-functionalism for the connectivist perspective as the theoretical power to drive us out of the confines of utilitarianism and discover an independent social system, the major contribution of conflict theory is its ability to lead us to find the dynamic force that creates, shapes, maintains and reforms the social system. In reality, conflict cannot be viewed as deviant, abnormal, and pathological while there is a functional order naturally out there. As David Lockwood pointed out, conflict is inevitable and inexorable. The societal mechanisms like power differentials assure a built-in tension in social systems. The groups with power and those without it constantly engage in fights over resources and societal goals.[6]

It has become clear that although conflict is not everything,[7] it is the dynamic force that promotes the creation, formation, and reformation of the social system. A theory that does not mention domination is one without the theoretical power to go beyond the understanding of the static status quo.

Conflict is inevitable when we are together, especially when we are forced together in an inescapable relationship like the international relationship. Each nation- state has to deal with it. We are generally prone to think of conflict as necessarily negative, as destructive of unity. But as Simmel emphasized many years ago, conflict can be positive in terms of integration and connection. The integrative function of conflict can be seen in subtle ways. As Simmel writes:

> Conflict itself resolves the tension between contrasts. The fact that it aims at peace is only one, an especially obvious, expression of its nature: the synthesis of elements that work both against and for one another. This nature appears more clearly when it is realized that both forms of relation—the antithetical and the convergent—are fundamentally distinguished from the mere indifference of two or more individuals or groups. Whether it implies the rejection or the termination of sociation, indifference is purely negative. In contrast to such pure negativity, conflict contains something positive. Its positive and negative aspects, however, are integrated; they can be separated conceptually, but not empirically.[8]

The origin of conflict theory is attributable to Karl Marx. However, as Arthur Stinchcombe insightfully points out, Marx is as much an evolutionist as a functionalist. There is much functional analysis in his arguments.[9] His theoretical point of departure is the functional need of the process of production. It is in this process that the force of productivity and the means and mode of production work as the driving forces in society and therefore shape other aspects of the society. Class struggle, which is viewed as the distinctive feature of Marxist conflict theory, is, in fact, the dynamic of social systems.

For Marx, it is the ruled class that is more dynamic in shaping the social system. He asserted that the politically ruled and economically exploited class, in the process of expanding and consolidating its newly developed mode of production, shapes the society around the specific type of their ownership of the means of production—they construct the legal system, the educational and religious system, and all the ideological constructions to safeguard their ownership of the means of production in a certain historical type and form. In this sense, this class is the most dynamic force in shaping the social system. For example, according to him, "The bourgeoisie, historically, has played a most revolutionary part."[10] But once it became the dominant and exploiting class, it is no longer revolutionary any more. The historical logic would shift the dynamics of social system from the bourgeoisie class to the proletariat class. By this logic, he predicts that the proletariat class will play the same revolutionary and historical role as the bourgeoisie did.

The key issue here is whether it was the interest-based bourgeoisie who were distinctive from the ruling elite group and played such a historical role or the relationship-based business people who worked as a part of the ruling elite social group and played such a historical role. This is more sociological than historical because it depends on how we understand the driving force in history that produced the historical change: interests or relationship? Georg Simmel is helpful in this respect.

For him, the unit of action is not class but rather the web of group affiliation. It has less to do with interests based on a certain mode of production, but is rather developed as an inseparable mingling associative and dissociative process.[11] He therefore shifts the focus from the economic or political division to social disconnection and its restoration. According to him, "Conflict is thus designed to resolve dualisms; it is a way of achieving some kind of unity, even if it be through the annihilation of one of the conflicting parties. This is roughly parallel to the fact that it is the most violent symptom of a disease which represents the effort of the organism to free itself of disturbances and damages caused by them."[12]

Unlike Marx, who viewed conflict as the vehicle for revolutionary structural change, Simmel saw conflict as a medium of integration, solidarity, and orderly change. For Marx, it is the class polarization that radically alters the system whole. But for Simmel, it is the level and mechanisms of organization that enable social systems to come into being. These mechanisms include conflict of low intensity and high frequency in system of high degrees of interdependence. Instead of intensifying or leading to radical structural change, they release tension and become normatively regulated. For example, in his *The philosophy of Money,*[13] he saw the conflict caused by using money, which includes quantifying social relationships, stimulating the division of labor, alienating workers further from the production process, etc. But unlike Marx, who condemned money because of its negative effects on capitalist society and looked for ways to eliminate these diseases in the future communist society, Simmel saw money as a social force to further integrate social system by providing more freedom to individuals. It is liberating and connecting instead of constraining and dividing. His conclusion is therefore that capitalism is self-transforming through the interaction of the social forces in the process of their struggle with each other. Liberation and connection occur as a gradual process when social forces intermingle. The forces that drive people's liberation and connection are not classes in the economic sense. They are social forces grounded in social associations and group affiliations.

The functional conflict theory enables us to think about an ancient but also very practical issue in almost all human relations: how can we possibly love our enemies? Here, we might understand this old Christian teaching about conflict through the functional lens. We have to love our enemies because they play important roles in our lives. We are willingly and, for the majority of the time, unwillingly, socially connected to our enemies. We have to live with this fact and the fact that the functions they play in our lives are essential for our development. Whoever can endure the painful functional conflicts among both lovers and enemies will come out strong. The people who are not strong enough to bear the burden of conflicts would not benefit from this structural arrangement of society.

The conclusion is clear: social world is highly dynamic and it moves in the direction of connection and integration; the driving force behind the dynamic process is constant and omnipresent conflict. In this way, Simmel brought the social force back in and highlighted the functions of social conflict between or among different social forces. "Web of group affiliations" is the key terms he used to describe this social force. But exactly what is the force of the web of group affiliations? How do we understand this type of social force? How does it work? The picture is a little blurry when we try to pinpoint this most dynamic force that shapes and maintains the social system. In recent decades, social network analysis has developed many powerful analytical tools to shape our intellectual thinking; it has also highlighted the dynamic social force that shapes and maintains social system.

A WORLD OF INTERCONNECTED UNITS OF ACTION

The key question network analysis answers is: what is the most powerful force in the social structure that both derives its power from the structure and shapes the structure? Power is the central concept of network analysis. However, it firmly grounds power in its location and connection to the overall social structure from which power is derived and exercised.[14] It views actors as points in an interconnected social system and describes the flow of events among actors. In the mean time, it has been moving in the direction of overcoming its initial drawback when it lacked of theoretical power to explain the dynamics of network structure.

In this way, network theory in sociology can highlight the idea of social forms in global affairs. This means that the true power of domestic politics is reflected by its embeddedness in social connections and that it has strong impact on national strength and its international competition. Network theory thus tells us to go beyond the macro perspective and envision the micro-macro interactions in social processes. It also highlights the importance of social forms, instead of content, in the process of creating and maintaining social structure. Among many contributions of this camp, the idea of exchange and the dependence relationships, the strength of weak ties, social capital, and structural hole are the most constructive ideas in terms of enlightening us about the genuine dynamics of global affairs.

Richard Emerson built up a solid foundation for network theory. He insightfully blends exchange theory and network analysis. He transplants the sophisticated discussion of power in exchange theory to the structural analysis in network theory and therefore produces a promising theoretical framework. After his tragic death, his colleague and collaborator Karen S. Cook has been carrying the torch and has furthered the discussion in this direction.[15]

For Emerson, the point of departure is his unit of analysis, which is the exchange relation between actors who are capable of conducting transactions (receiving and bestowing gratifications to and from others). The analysis is therefore shifted away from actors themselves and their attributes. The goal is to understand the patterns of relations, the relational unit. He emphasizes three major concepts, which are power, dependence, and balance. According to him, dependence is a situation where an actor's capability to receive gratification is contingent upon the behaviors of another actor. If the degree of dependence of actor A on actor B equals the degree of dependence of actor B on actor A, there is a balance. If actor A can force actor B to incur costs because of the unbalanced degree of dependence of B on A, the issue of power arises. Actor A therefore has a power advantage over actor B. The other two concepts, alternatives and uncertainty, also play a role here. The more alternatives actor A has, the less dependent he has to be on actor B. The more uncertainty he experiences, the more dependent he has to be on other actors. However, the exchange transactions tend to balance the unbalanced relationship.

Based on these basic assumptions, Emerson developed several basic social forms as the structure of networks. The first one is unilateral monopoly, in which actor A possesses the source of valuable resources while actors B1, B2, and B3 are dependent on actor A for these resources. As the relationship goes on for a period of time, the Bs will eventually shift the power dynamics by either reducing the value of the resources they receive from A, finding an alternative, or forming a coalition to negotiate better terms. However, the ultimate measure to balance the relationship is the emergence of a division of labor among the Bs. So the second form Emerson developed is division of labor. In a situation of division of labor, Bs would become specialized in their exchange relationships with A—each B provides A with different values in exchange for his monopolized resources. In this way, each B will become monopolized in certain ways so the degree of dependence of A on each B will increase.

The third form is social circle and its stratification. Action units with similar resources or value tend to cluster together to form networks. Once their

circle is closed, a stratification system will emerge based on the crystalliza-
tion of the social circles.

The last form developed by Emerson and Cook is the dynamics of centrality. Centrality is viewed as one of the most important terms of a network
analysis. It indicates the location of a point (an action unit), its distance to the
center, and how it connects to other points. Cook uses Emerson's idea to develop a hypothesis that highlights the power dynamics of centrality. According to this hypothesis, as points increases in the network, connections increase. The power will shift from the center of the entire network to the points
where most connections are developed. The point that has the most connection is in the position to monopolize the most resources.

In conclusion, the dynamics of the social system as it is described by
Emerson and Cook are from bottom up. It is the balancing power of the disadvantaged actors that eventually balances the unbalanced relationship.
However, they did not make clear the source of power of the disadvantaged
actors. A key issue is the dominant power of the advantaged actors. If someone has the sufficient resource to generate enough dependency between
himself and others, he is more likely to have sufficient power to safeguard
his position and resources. Another issue beyond the exchange-resource
perspective is that relations themselves are resources. If someone has already possessed sufficient relations to occupy a central position in the network, it is less likely for him to leave too much space for others to force him
become a mere figurehead.

Both Putnam and Skocpol used the network approach to discuss the significance of community construction and development on the civic side of the
political system.[16] However, I would argue that Granovetter's model, the
strength of weak ties, has made this point more clearly.[17] According to him,

> people rarely act on mass-media information unless it is also transmitted
> through personal ties; otherwise one has no particular reason to think that an ad-
> vertised product or an organization should be taken seriously." "Trust in leaders
> is integrally related to the capacity to predict and affect their behavior. Leaders,
> for their part, have little motivation to be responsive or even trustworthy toward
> those to whom they have no direct or indirect connection. Thus, network frag-
> mentation, by reducing drastically the number of paths from any leader to his
> potential followers, would inhibit trust in such leaders. This inhibition, further-
> more, would not be entirely irrational.[18]

Also, according to Granovetter, a sign of powerlessness is a lack of weak
ties as resources at their disposal. This is especially true among working class
people because of their simple work and lifestyles and their closer involvement in few strong ties.[19]

The concept of "strength of weak ties" originally intended to shed light on the impact of the closeness of interpersonal social connections on individuals. It further demonstrated that the strength of social ties, an important form of social relationship, plays a big role in shaping social structure in general. It further leads us the idea of social capital, which means social relations have value; to develop social relationship is a value-added process. It highlights that the amount, type, and strength of social connections can be effective indicators of how much capital an individual possesses, just like money or assets can be used to measure a person's financial capital, and education and work experiences can be used to measure human capital. Here social capital is similar to the notion of "social power" as it is contrasted to material power, institutional power, and cultural power.[20]

Ronald Burt's concept "structural hole" offers a powerful indicator and measure of relational power in structured social connections. Its key idea is that the people who are socially functional in between related but distinctively structured webs of institutional or interpersonal ties possess the most power.[21] It is significant in that it has corrected a conventional notion that power is exclusively rooted in separated human communities. Since we are used to the tribalistic way of thinking, we usually regard "bonding" within our own community is the way to power. But Burt shows us that "bridging" between human communities is more powerful and effective in terms of obtaining and expanding power. "Structural hole" bestows its occupants the positional and relational advantages when they compete with the localized "within-the-structure" people.

Nan Lin developed a comprehensive theory on social capital. His theory can be summarized as the followings:

First, he answered a key question about the formation of social structure as a whole. Why is social structure (group and collectivity) not only possible, but inevitable from rational action and interaction principles? How do "interdependent individual actions produce system (or collective) level outcomes?"[22]

Nan Lin developed two propositions to establish this connection between individual rational choice and social structure. They are as the followings:

> The accumulation of social capital is much faster than that of human capital. That is, accumulation of human capital tends to be additive in nature, whereas accumulation of social capital tends to be exponential.

> When interaction outside of one's primordial group are intended to gain resource, they are used more for accessing social capital than gaining human capital.[23]

Human capital expansion is the most familiar form in human history. But it is limited by an insurmountable difficulty: the strict requirement for the

scarce and vital resources (food, as well as all the other materials) to physically sustain those humans. Also, managing and controlling both the human
resource and the natural resources that sustain human resource can be more
and more difficult as the size of the group grows . The ultimate source of war
and enslavement is the struggle for human capital expansion. But marginal
utility would be dramatically reduced as soon as the group reaches certain
size beyond the ability of management. On the contrary, the social capital expansion does not have to deal with such a difficulty. The key issue is that we
do not have to own it but we can still use it, as long as we commit our own
resources as well (reciprocity).[24] This is the reason why human capital expansion is additive whereas social capital expansion is exponential.

The benefit of social capital can therefore be illustrated as:

> Social capital is generated by creating and maintaining social ties. A relation
> with a social tie suggests a linkage and therefore access to the tie's resources:
> social capital for ego. Further, once a tie is accessed, not only do his or her re-
> source become social capital to ego, but the alter's social ties also offer possible
> social capital. As these ties extend into a network of both direct and indirect ties,
> the pool of social capital grows exponentially.[25]

The multiplicity of the individual drive for weaving interpersonal ties produces social structure. "A collectivity is an aggregation of actors and primor-
dial groups bound together for the sharing of social capital."[26] More rewards
and power are given to those who demonstrate a high degree of loyalty and/or
a high level of performance. Leadership is manifested in a form of enforcing
agency whereas free riders are punished by being placed on the low positions
in the hierarchy. Power and authority are established in this social process of
networking and connection. A hierarchical system is therefore formed as the
social structure.[27]

Nan Lin then answered another key question: Why would someone higher
in social position and richer in resources be willingly to engage in repeated
exchanges with someone lower in social position and poorer in resources?[28]

Nan Lin answered this question by contrasting two types of rationality:
transactional rationality and relational rationality. "Relational rationality favors the maintenance and promotion of the relationship even when the transactions are less than optimal. Transactional rationality favors the optimal outcome of transactions even if it is necessary to terminate specific relations."[29]

The essence of pursuing transactional gains is visible market force (money)
with calculable profits whereas the essence of pursuing relational gains is
semi-visible relationships and invisible and incalculable power of social control. Nan Lin therefore laid out the rational choices about the alternatives under each rationality: under transactional rationality, people change partners

and relationships if it is not profitable; under relational rationality, people can only change transactions if it hurts relationships—terminating relationship with partners is not beneficial. Especially for the people on the higher positions, they "depend on the survival, persistence, and, indeed, ever-expanding nature of social circle, to sustain and promote their social standing."[30] It is the survival of the strongest and smartest on the market place that drives behind the dynamics of transactional rationality; whereas it is the survival of the most connected in the persistent social relationships that drives behind the dynamics of relational rationality.

It is clear that the two rationalities are not compatible. Based on transactional rationality, people on the higher positions with more resources would have less incentive to develop and maintain relationships with the less resourceful people on the lower positions. Under transactional rationality, it does not make sense to start or keep a relationship if it is not profitable, since people and relationship are only accidental and unimportant whereas transactional gains are paramount. However, based on relational rationality, people on the higher positions with more resources would have high motivation to develop and maintain relationships with the people on the lower positions. The reason is clear: social relationships matter the most to them. The survival of their social status depends on their leadership positions in the web of social ties.[31]

One of the applications of this network approach is my research on the Watergate Affair and my conclusion about the American political system.[32] The strength of the American political system is reflected by the so-called "Washington Collective Power Dynamic" in which the formally institutionalized political system is embedded in informal social connections through the appropriate strength of social ties and the sufficient amount of social capital among powerful politicians in Washington. However, the weakness of the American political system is also reflected by its lack of weak social ties between political elites and ordinary citizens. The network understanding of domestic politics provides a powerful tool to make sense of and predict national strength in a "social" way. It helps us to determine a nation's strength by measuring the amount of social capital, the strength of social ties, and the structural advantage (or disadvantage) it possesses.

In terms of global politics, network theory can help us further understand the "social power" approach. This is an essential step for us to go beyond realism (hard power) and liberalism (soft power) and develop a third and possibly more effective way to grasp the genuine nature of global power dynamics. The social forms envisioned by network theory are important manifestations of social connections and social dynamics because they do not focus on contents which are conventionally regarded as economical and political interests.

More importantly, elite social groups are naturally pushed to compete against each other to gain a broader and deeper social reach. But there are social factors that would determine the success or failure of their competition for social power. These social factors include their structural positions in the webs of social connections within and among nations, and their institutionalized strategies based on their cultural heritage. For example, it might be more effective to pursue weak ties in global politics, but since the institutionalized way of social connection for a specific elite social group is to focus on strong ties, the group as a whole or the leaders of the elite group might consciously or unconsciously concentrate their energy and resources on ineffective strong ties. All of these social powers are essential for an elite social group's status on a global scale and affect the global status of the general population under its control as well.

THE CONNECTIVE POWER DYNAMICS

General

The Deweyan notion of the three levels of social understanding is the epistemological foundation of the concept of connective power dynamics. According to Dewey, there are three levels of social understanding. The first one is self-action: "Where things are viewed as acting under their own powers." The second level is inter-action: "Where thing is balanced against thing in causal interconnection."[33] However, the highest level is transaction:

> Where systems of description and naming are employed to deal with aspects and phases of action, without final attribution to "elements" or other presumptively detachable or independent "entities," or "essences," or "realities," and without isolation of presumptively detachable "relations" from such detachable "elements."[34]

The idea of social embeddedness can best bridge the Deweyan epistemology and my synthesis about sociological understanding of global power dynamics. It was first developed in the field of the sociological research on business organizations.[35] The initial idea is that in order to achieve a better understanding of business organizations and business operations, we will have to enclose them closely in their social surroundings and regard them as integral and inseparable parts of their social environments. In my study of the Watergate Affair and the American political system, I further extended the application of this concept to an understanding of political systems. I further regard political systems as integral parts of the social system. We cannot understand a political system without uncovering the social dynamics of the society at large. The types of social connections, i.e. the strength and extent of social ties, are the essence of power relationships, more important than formal political constructions.[36] Here, the concept of social embeddedness plays an analytical role in the integration of the ideas from seemingly conflicting schools in sociology and the ability to piece them together to form a coherent new theory. This theory includes the concept of social functioning from the structural-functionalist school, the idea of elite dominance and class struggle from the conflict school, and the ideas of social capital, strength of social ties, and "structure hole." Together, they defy and falsify the conventional theory of individualistic rational choice and demystify the notion of material and institutional powers. Social reach and social connectedness are the catch phrases of this new theoretical synthesis. I would like to term it "social connectivism."

This theory regards social system as a distinctive arena which is independent from political or economic fields. The basic structure of this system is institutionalized roles and behavior patterns which are embedded in and work through webs of networks. The basic unit of action is interpersonal/international ties. The key concept of this theory is "connective power dynamics." It highlights the theoretical judgment about a good match or mismatch about individuals' behavior pattern and their positions in the institutionalized web of their social ties. Society, or social system, is shaped by these empowered or disempowered individuals in this type of unit of action. The theory therefore reveals the deep-seated social dynamics inside the societal institutional construction. It emphasizes the issue of the social embeddedness of political institutions. Therefore it points out the direction of the social process of power construction and power dynamics in the social system as a whole.

Connective power dynamics play a significant role in the social system. It works as an effective bridge to connect the society as a whole. But generally speaking, the institutionalized parts of the social system are embedded in formal organizations with limited connective power, which would confine the system to national borders. The formal institutions are not capable of effectively connecting the entire global society. As a result, even inside national borders, they are often superficial and ineffective. We need to fully develop a connective power to genuinely connect the global social system as an organic whole. Lack of weak ties between the powerful and the less powerful might be the major problem that inhibits the genuine connection of the social system and harms the cohesiveness of the social process. It is thus a major cause of global fragmentation.

Therefore, the connective approach might enable us to find the source of the strength of a global social system. It might help us to answer: How could the system involve more and more action units into its process but at the same time guarantee its stability and healthy operation? How could a genuine connection be built up between the powerful insiders and marginalized outsiders? For those excluded from the process of the system, how could we help them develop the weak ties if the lack of weak ties constitutes the major hurdle for them to gain access to the system? How could we clearly utilize all the subtle but powerful social dynamics to facilitate the genuine connection in the global social system? The key point here is that, for a society in general and for a political system in particular, the more weak ties among different kinds of action units, especially between those with power and those without much power, the better. The key issue is to institutionalize more channels and paths that would facilitate and nourish the development and growth of more and more weak ties among all action units in the social system.

In the international field, it is the relational web which is the fundamental structure of world order and change. When individual nation-states construct their interests and develop strategies to pursue those interests, the most effective way is to look for relationships first. There is no fixed and predetermined national interest without referencing it to specific social relationships. Because of the issue of social power, relationships are paramount and more valuable than specific interests.

This theoretical construction also enables us to answer a fundamental question in international politics. What is the source of power? I depart from most neo-realists at this point because I believe the sources of power include but are not limited to material forces. An important source of power is social capital—how many accumulated connections we have with other nation-states and how effectively these connections work in a meaningful way.

Furthermore, I view the established institutions as the condensation of rich social relationships. It is emphasized that the roles and rules, as well as functional structures, of international institutions are all embedded in certain social relationships among nation-states. However, once they are formed and established, they become relatively independent forces with high possibility to shape the social relationships in which they are embedded.

Last but not least, relationships would not work without power. I am a realist in this sense because I do not focus on norms or ideals. Instead, I regard power and interests as the driving forces in international society. Therefore, sociological conflict theory and realism and neo-realism in the field of international relations play an important role in terms of shaping the idea of "connective power dynamics." I have no quarrel with the point that people, or nation-states, are driven by their interests and it is their structural power that enables their activities. Structured power distribution is the only dynamic force in international relations. What I would like to highlight is how their interests are developed and what is the key component of power.

"Connective"

The whole idea is about connectiveness. It has been taken for granted that the term "individual" means a totally separated self, persons or nations alike, with a boundary between one and another. According to this construction of self, a social entity is viewed as a "container" and as a "bounded, unique, more or less integrated motivational and cognitive universe, a dynamic center of awareness, emotion, judgment, and action organized into a distinctive whole and set contrastively both against other such wholes and against a social and natural background."[37]

This "self," characterized by individualism, exhibits a firm self-contained self-other boundary. Barring unhealthy symbiosis, other "selves" are not an intrinsic part of constructing oneself.[38] Although the independent self must exhibit "relatedness," in the sense of being responsive to the social environment and to social situations in general, adaptation to, and awareness of, these social constraints derives from the need to verify and affirm the inner core of the self.[39]

A nation means a separated and detached group of people with a clearly marked boundary that separates them from other similar nations. Within the boundary, we see unified economic, political, legal, military, and educational systems that distinguish this group of people from others. These separated groups of people therefore have distinctive interpretations of their self-interests and are propelled by their clearly understood interpretations of national interests.

Set out from the Deweyan notion of the transactional reality, it is safe to say that everything is connected to everything else. The connective nature of social reality is reflected by the manner in which individuals as unit of action are always socially included in each other. They are "aspect" of the whole. The socially inclusive "self" defines all individuals as a self-in-relation-to-others rather than a thoroughly self-contained, separated entity. "Self" is constructed through the web of relationships to which individual social "entities" owe a continuing, and probably life-time, dependence—a dependence not only in an external social-economic sense, but also, and more importantly, a cognitive and emotional dependence. Individual social "entities" would not exist if they could not be inseparable with webs of social relationships. Therefore, social "entities" are in fact social "aspects" of a system to which they are not detachable.

The potency of this perspective is in the significance of these webs of connective ties for the growth of modern nations. Essential national institutions, e.g., banks, insurance companies, manufacturers, educational organizations, health care providers, as well as political institutions—are all parts of globally developed webs of connective ties. Their very existence depends on similar institutional constructions in other nations across the globe. It is the global process of networking, specialization and inclusion that made these institutions possible. They are not independent and detachable from the global system. And it is clear that without uniting, including, and integrating the very inner core of these institutions through social and professional relations beyond national borders, nations would not exist at all. The world would have long been a chaotic Leviathan and therefore would have ceased to exist long before we were able to talk about it today.

In this view, a nation devoid of global relatedness has little meaningful content of its own, since the nations could only be understood in terms of webs of connective ties on the global scale. A nation is seen predominantly as an "aspect" whose basic task is uniting its material and spiritual well-being to the limitless and ubiquitous global webs of connective ties. The uniqueness of each nation is mostly manifest by the degree of this kind of unification within a ceaseless process of broadening and deepening webs of relationships. Therefore, a nation is never conceived of as an isolated or isolatable entity. The catch phrases for the global system might be "togetherness" and "inclusiveness."

"Power Dynamics"

However, this reality has not undermined the autonomy of individual nations. In the inseparable web based system, a nation is constantly in a painful state because of its unique ways of feeling and the desire constructed by its unique history and its distinctive contemporary domestic structure. Power comes into play at this point. It is the unitary link between aspiration and instrument of the nations that facilitates their international power. But each nation that is linked in the chain of international power dynamics checks others with high degree of autonomy through countless webs of connections. Everyone is an instrument of others, while at the same time being the aspiration of others. In this tight web, it is very easy to imagine a tension, the tension between the globally shaped collective way, the often submerged unitary psyche of all nations' webs-of-belonging, and the individual nation's unique group feelings and desires.

The classic definition of power, as it stated by Max Weber and Robert Dahl, is the ability to make others do what they otherwise would not do—to make others do what we want them to do regardless of their resistance.[40] I accept this definition in order to analyze international power dynamics. However, I would like to add a scope condition to it. Power is always relational;

it can only be materialized in a world of connectiveness. Here, where the strive for independence and detachability would weaken a nation's position in the international system, the strong push of connection is to transform individualistic/nationalistic feelings and desires from separated and isolated unique systems to being a specific part of the global web. It should be counterproductive if anyone tries to cure the pain by building an even more unique and isolated national identity and institution. Here we see the mechanism of the connective social reality as the scope condition of power.

Realists in the field of international relations always argue with the Thucydides' notion that "the strong do what they can and the weak suffer what they must."[41] This assertion is true to a certain extent, but it overlooks the relational aspect that the strong can only become strong when they can successfully connect to the weak. They can do little in a gated community. In the mean time, the weak are weak not necessarily because of their material strength; rather, it is very likely that they are weak because they connect to the world in a wrong way. The realist notion also overlooks a functionally dynamic process. The fact that the strong can do what they can is more based on their structural position and less on their material capabilities. Only after a nation itself is shaped by its structural position through successfully connecting to the world as a whole can it successfully develop its capability and exercise it accordingly. Here we see the dynamics between the strong and the weak. The strong exercise power over the weak by their relational and functional ability to impose their will upon the weak despite the latter's resistance. Since this can only happen in a connected global structure, for both the strong and the weak, the process is painful. Because they would have to reshape themselves according to the relational and functional structure.

However, this painful process is not necessarily bad for the nations that suffer from the pain. Under these circumstances, only when a nation successfully transforms its individual national feelings and desires to a level that enable it to shape and fit in the unitary psyche of its web, and makes the two undetachable, can it become a "real leader." Nations bring their individual strengths to the global web and they are only strong if they construct their uniqueness towards contributing something specific to the web. A real leader is not only normatively upstanding and legally sound, but also the "fittest" in the web of its belonging. Its strength is developed and maintained by its ability to put its strong individuality into the constructive and positive functioning of the web as a whole. This is not only the best way for the more constructive internal national development, but also the best way to maximize its external interests. The external criteria of the transformation are: loyal devotion to the causes which are related as the "web interests" and commitment to the ties in the webs. At the same time, each time an individual nation violates these principles, it will be punished by weakening its position in the web and thus, losing more interests.

I hope I have made it clear that we are not discussing norms or values. We are not talking about what a world "should" be. Instead, I am trying to convey the idea of what the world is. This connective system is very realistic, ubiquitous, and profound in each nation's daily life. It would have strong impact on all nations, regardless of whether they seek leadership positions or not. It pushes profound internal change and transformation within these nations as well. Indeed, it could surely make many people in these nations unhappy and make the process of internal transformation painful. But, it could also force a nation to control its selfish and often self-destructive pursuits. It also conforms to a "socially selective" law, i.e., that if a nation is constantly weakening the web of its belonging by its narrow-minded behavior, it is apparent that it cannot bear the burden of taking care of others and the global collective interests. In this case, it may be simply forced to stay in a lower status of the web and obtain less benefit from the connective ties. A nation becomes strong and capable of exercising power only when it can be the carrier of part of the broad web. At the same time, it could obtain full support from the web for most of its efforts. In this way, its national power would get legitimized and it would gain the high status to command the obedience of other nations.

It would be the case that the more you belong to the global web and the more important functions you are able to play, the more other nations would belong to you. On the other hand, the stronger you are in the connective system, the more impact you would be able to have on the connective web. Individual nations are not valued by their natural rights as sovereign nations, but instead, by their degrees of functioning to the web as a whole and by their contributions to the development and maintenance of the global web of connective ties. The strong and influential individual nation's interests are more likely to be synonymous with the interests of all the nations on the broad global web because of the inclusive nature of the connective system.

In this sense, the global web appears to be a rather hierarchical and contradictory social relationship. It is oftentimes a coercive one in nature. Conflicts on all fronts are universal and constant. It is important to note that social conflicts, instead of being destructive, work as the major dynamic for the functioning of existing international institutions and for the balance of power. It is the effective way for the weak to express and develop themselves and the way for the strong to maintain their strength. Through social conflicts, the weak are able to constantly contest the strong and push for their niche of becoming stronger. It is through social conflict that the genuine balance of power reveals itself.

It is also because of the connective nature of global affairs that another point could be made: no power is invincible. Power is a very relative "aspect" of the connective system. It depends on who and what it is dealing with. A very powerful military machine with formalized organization and solid supply system might not be so powerful when it has to deal with a guerrilla warfare that is organized in a form of informal networks and needs only minimal material supplies. A strong economy might be very vulnerable when it is hit by a wide-spread pandemic or serious environmental crises. Therefore, the connective global process requires everyone, including the seemingly most powerful one, to share vulnerability based upon the principle of mutuality. A global leader must be one that gains its acceptance through mutuality and sharing vulnerability.

I share with Kenneth Waltz his emphasis on structure. But my structure is different from his. For him, it is the structure of the distribution of capabilities among nation-states and nation-states play similar functions in the global structure; for me, it is the structure of the connective ties among nation-states and nation-states play different functions in terms of maintaining the structure. Capabilities can only be developed through functional role playing and framed in the structure of connective ties.

In sum, politically and organizationally, the global web as a connective system transforms individual nations into "aspects" of an organic global system. Every individual nation is therefore pushed to make efforts to become more powerful and functional, not in the sense of self-action and self-propelling, but in the web by including others in its national development. In this case, the energy of the entire global web could be mobilized to overcome some difficulties which an individual nation, however powerful it might be, could not bear alone. This connective system would produce an attractive system for the strong nations and a less oppressive one for the weak nations. The strong are motivated to sustain the weak, in part through the responsibilities of taking care of the whole web; the weak may obtain some power from the web through mutuality and sharing vulnerability.

In the process of globalization, socio-economic institutions that overlap with an extended and stable web of socially connected ties among most nations are developing. Therefore, a web of connective ties on the global scale would become stronger and more able to reach out and to influence a broader spectrum of behavior, including political practices. Therefore, connective power dynamics based upon this connective global system would become more and more decisive in international politics. A system of global governance would therefore take shape.

As we all well know, governance is based upon authority. In the field of international studies, we see many discussions about power, but many fewer about authority. However, in reality, without a system of legitimated power, it would be impossible to talk about a governance system. The next chapter sets out to outline a concept of authority that is derived from the notion of connective power dynamics. I term this type of authority "connective."

NOTES

1. Jonathan H. Turner, *The Structure of Social Theory*, fourth edition (Chicago, Ill. The Dorsey Press, 1986).

2. Emile Durkheim, *The Division of Labor in Society*, trans. G. Simpson (New York: Free Press, 1964).

3. Talcott Parsons, "The Present Position and Prospect of Systemic Theory in Sociology." *Essays in Sociological Theory* (New York: Free Press, 1949), 229.

4. Talcott Parsons, *Social System* (New York: Free Press, 1951).

5. Talcott Parsons, Robert F. Bales, and Edward A Shils, *Working Papers in the Theory of Action* (Glencoe, Ill. Free Press, 1953).

6. David Lockwood, "Some Remarks on 'The Social System." *British Journal of Sociology* 7, (June 1956):134–146.

7. For a diverse sample of different theoretical orientations within the conflict framework, see William Gamson, *The Strategy of Social Protest* (Homewood, Ill.: Dorsey Press, 1975); Randall Collins, *Conflict Sociology* (New York: Academic Press, 1975); James Coleman, *Community Conflict* (Glencoe Ill.: Free Press, 1957); Thomas C. Shelling, *The Strategy of Conflict* (Cambridge MA: Harvard University Press, 1960).

8. Arthur L. Stinchcombe, *Constructing Social Theories* (New York: Hartcourt, Brace, & World, 1968).

9. Karl Marx and Friedrich Engels, *Manifesto of the Communist Party,* in *The Marx-Englels Reader*, second edition, ed. Robert C. Tucker (New York: W.W Norton, 1978).

10. Georg Simmel, *Conflict and the Web of Group Affiliation*, trans. Kurt H. Wolff and Reinhard Bendix (New York: Free Press, 1955).

11. Simmel, 1955, 13, 14.

12. Georg Simmel, *The Philosophy of Money* (Boston: Routledge & Kegan Paul, 1978).

13. Simmel, 1955, 14.

14. For some basic reference on network analysis, see Peter Marsden and Nan Lin, eds. *Social Structure and Network Analysis* (Beverly Hills, CA.: Sage Publications, 1982); Berry Wellman, "Network Analysis: Some Basic Principles," *Sociological Theory*,1, (1983): 155–200; Ronald Burt, 1982, *Toward a Structural Theory of Action: Network Models of Social Structure, Perception and Action* (New York: Academic Press, 1982); John Scott, 2000, *Social Network Analysis—a handbook,* second edition (London: Sage Publications, 2000).

15. Richard Emerson "Power-Dependence Relations," *American Sociological Review,* 17, (Feb. 1962): 31–41; "Power-Dependence Relations: Two Experiments," *Sociometry,* (27 Sept. 1964): 282–98; John F. Stolte and Richard M. Emerson, "Structural Inequality: Position and Power in Network Structures," in *Behavioral Theory in Sociology,* ed. R. Hamblin (New Brunswick, N.J.: Transaction Book, 1977); Karen S. Cook and Richard Emerson, "Power, Equity and Commitment in Exchange Networks," *American Sociological Review,* Vol. 43, (1978): 712–39; Karen S. Cook, Richard M. Emerson, Mary R. Gillmore, and Toshio Yamagish, "The Distribution of Power in Exchange Networks," *American Journal of Sociology,* Vol. 89, (1983): 275–305; Karen S.Cook, "Exchange and Power in Networks of Interorganizational Relations," *Sociological Quarterly,* No. 18, (Winter 1977): 66–82; Karen S. Cook and Karen A. Hegtvedt, "Distributive Justice, Equity, and Equality," *American Sociological Review* 39, (1983): 217–41.

16. Robert D. Putnam, *Bowling Alone: the collapse and revival of American Community* (New York: Simon and Schuster, 2000); Theda Skocpol, *Diminished Democracy: from membership to management in American civil life* (Norman: University of Oklahoma Press, 2003).

17. Granovetter, Mark. "The Strength of Weak Ties" *American Journal of Sociology* 78, No.6, (1973): 1360–1380; "Economic Action and Social Structure: the problem of embeddedness" *American Journal of Sociology* 91, No.3, (1985): 481–510.

18. Mark Granovetter, 1973: 1374.

19. Mark Granovetter, "The Theory-Gap in Social Network Analysis," in Paul Holland and Samuel Leinhardt, eds. *Perspectives on Social Network Research* (New York: Academic Press, 1979); "The Strength of Weak Ties: A Network Theory Revisited," *Sociological Theory,* No.1, (1983): 201–33.

20. Robert D. Putnam, 2000; Nan Lin, *Social Capital—a theory of social structure and action* (New York: Cambridge University Press, 2001).

21. Ronald S. Burt, *Structure Holes; the social structure of competition,* (Cambridge, MA: Harvard University Press, 1992).

22. Nan Lin, 127.

23. Nan Lin, 134.

24. Nan Lin, 134–135.

25. Nan Lin, 134–135.

26. Nan Lin, 137.

27. Nan Lin, 137–139.

28. Nan Lin, 143.

29. Nan Lin, 150.

30. Nan Lin, 156.

31. Nan Lin, 154-158.

32. Tian-jia Dong, 2005, *Understanding Power through Watergate: the Washington collective power dynamics,* Lanham, MD: University Press of America.

33. John Dewey & Arthur F. Bentley, *Knowing and the Known,* in *Useful procedures of Inquiry,* edited by Rollo Handy and E.C. Harwood (Behavior Research Council, Great Barrington, MA, 1973): 121.

34. Dewey and Bentley: 121-122.

35. Paul DiMaggio and Hugh Louch. "Social Embedded Consumer Transactions: for what kinds of purchases do people most often use networks?" *American Sociological Review* 63 (October 1998): 619–637.

36. Tian-jia Dong, 2005, "Conclusion".

37. Clifford Geertz, "On the Nature of Anthropological Understanding," *American Scientist:* 63 (1975): 48.

38. Steven Johnson, *Humanizing the Narcissistic Style* (New York: W.W. Norton, 1987).

39. Hazel Markus & S. Kitayama, "Culture and the Self: implications for cognition, emotion, and motivation." *Psychological Review* Vol. 98, No.2 (1991); Dongxiao Qin, "Toward a Critical Feminist Perspective of Culture and Self," *Feminism & Psychology*, Vol. 14, No. 2 (2004): 297–312.

40. Max Weber, *Economy and Society*, Cambridge, MA: Harvard University Press, 1954): 323; Robert Dahl, "The Concept of Power," *Behavioral Science* 2 (1957)

41. Thucydides, *Book V.* paragraph 90, chapter XVII, (Modern Library Edition): 31

Chapter Three

The Connective Authority

ESTABLISHING A GLOBAL AUTHORITY SYSTEM

It is obvious that as the process of globalization becomes prevailing, the world needs a global order. Individual nations do not necessarily follow the same rules and a chaotic international situation is likely to endanger the entire human existence. This logic would lead us to see the necessity of exploring the issue of an effective system of global governance. To govern means to lead. An effective leadership must be powerful and at the same time constructive. Therefore, powerful states are not automatically functioning as leaders. Leaders must possess acceptability. Theoretically, this is an issue of how power can be transformed into authority. A very practical question emerges: how is it possible that one sovereign nation follows another?

It is clear that the power factor plays a big role here. But, as we all well know, power cannot guarantee willing follower. The powerful must undertake one or more of the following three actions in order to secure followers. The first action is to punish those who choose not to follow. The second is to reward those who choose to follow. Both of these actions, as we can see throughout human history, are very costly. Wars are risky and expensive; economic sanctions would inflict long-term damage to all the parties involved. Purchasing followers has never been cheap; it is also unreliable and difficult. So the third way becomes significant: it is the action of seeking legitimacy in international interactions. Legitimacy can smoothly transform raw power into acceptable authority by securing willing acceptance of power on the part of the less powerful.

A more practical question follows: how can American leadership be more effective and, at the same time, more acceptable across the globe? The United

States of America has been the only global superpower since the end of the Cold War and the only nation that has the capability to carry on full fledged global duties and to safeguard a global order. It is the only nation-state that has the potential political power to facilitate global social control and the economic resources to help other nation-states deal with issues of production and consumption worldwide. However, its power did not automatically bring sufficient willing followers to it thus far. The US has had to use all the three means mentioned above for the purpose of creating and maintaining its global dominance. However, this effort has not been so successful to this point. The key problem is the incompatibility of the object role America has been playing and its subjective consciousness about it. Since there is no clear understanding about the objective role, the nation squandered its leadership opportunity by overlooking its objective position and neglecting its functional role. Trapped in the very costly Iraq war, threatened by waves of global terrorism, and facing uncontrollable defiance, even resentment, from all corners of the globe, the US needs to rethink its global strategy for its leadership. And needless to say, the best action is to take the third way—to go the highroad by focusing on establishing the legitimacy of American leadership. But this is definitely not an easy task. The legitimacy crisis of American power since the Iraq War highlighted this point very clearly.

In the 2000 presidential campaign, President Bush declared that the United States would gain respect and attraction if it were strong and, at the same time, "humble." Here Bush had a keen instinct, but this was more easily said than done. The difficulty in being humble is that the policy makers in the US firmly believe that, to use President Bill Clinton's words, the US is a "beacon of hope to peoples around the world." Therefore, by acting alone as an all powerful benign hegemon, the US would naturally bring peace, prosperity and security to the world.

With this kind of mentality, it would be hard not to behave arrogantly. "Humbleness" cannot be superficial gestures. It requires that the actor understand the deep-seated social mechanism of global governance. To transform the US superpower into legitimized global authority, the policy makers in the US must adopt a new way of thinking by understanding the nature of authority. Here, some theoretical guidance is obviously necessary.

CONNECTIVE AUTHORITY DEFINED

In the field of international studies, there are many talks about power but many fewer about authority. For realism, power is the key; authority in terms of legitimated power is not so important. Liberalism, although there much talk about soft power and legitimacy is regarded as the core of international order and dynamics, does not offer much theoretical insight in terms of understanding international authority. If we accept the significance of connective power dynamics, the concept of authority reveals to us more about the nature of international relations because it is connective in nature. In daily international interactions, power without acceptance or legitimacy does exist and is highly prevailing. But it is much less likely to do the power-holder any good in a long run and therefore it is not likely to be effective in terms of shaping an international governance system. On the contrary, authority is harder to exercise but it is much more enduring and effective. A global governance system is more dependent on authority than power in this sense. When we try to rescue political power from pure political institutions and embed it in social relationships, it is essential to transform "power" into "authority."

Max Weber offered a classic sociological understanding of power and authority. His major contributions are his definition of the concept of power (as we discussed in Chapter 2), his linkage between power and authority, and his three ideal types of authority. For Max Weber, politics mean "striving to share power or striving to influence the distribution of power, either among states or among groups within a state."[1] However, Weber has gone one step further by answering a key question: how is it possible for a large assemblage of individuals (persons or other units of action) to accept the distribution of power one way or another? In another word, how is politics legitimized? Weber avowed that ruler cannot rule without the willing or unwilling obedience of their subordinates. Power without authority is sheer domination which cannot sustain for long if it cannot somehow create compliance one way or another. In international politics, a strong nation which exercises power without making effective efforts to create authority is no different from a school-yard bully who might force others to bend to his will for a while; sheer force will be balanced sooner rather than later. Any individualistic understanding about power for power's sake is incomplete and unhelpful.

As defined by Max Weber, authority is the legitimated or accepted power. The precondition for authority is that there must be at least two sides and they must connect to each other. Weber offered a partial connection between the political and the social through his three types of authority—the traditional, rational-legal and charismatic. Power, therefore, is no longer solely rooted in individualistic and pure political constructions.

This book goes beyond Max Weber. It presents "connective authority" as a new concept and analyzes its application to international relations. By referring to the discussion of the dynamic and transforming power of social connections, this book regards connective authority as a higher level of authority which is poised to include the Weberian three ideal types at the lower order, under the two new types. The discussion departs from power as functional roles and social ties in interpersonal and international activities.

Connective authority is therefore constructed as follows:

1. Individual power can only be legitimated through certain type of relationships. Connective authority is generated by omnipresent and preexisting connections: since we all live in and through the inescapable relationship, we must work through others if we set out to create compliance, no matter how powerful we are. The inseparability of the seemingly independent units bestows legitimacy to the powerful in the relational web who are most connected.
2. Power is legitimized because of its social connection to the less powerful or powerless as an "aspect" of a system. Acceptable dominance and willing obedience only happen when they are inseparable from and undetachable to a Deweyan sense transactional system. Therefore, neither of them is driven by the self-action of independent actors. Whereas power is a decisive factor here, it is only accepted as a part of an inseparable system.
3. Individual actors' dominance or obedience is legitimized by the co-presence of the following two factors: first is their special ways of connection to others in the connective system; second is their institutionalized and specialized positions in the system. The former is established through seemingly fussy webs of network ties and the latter through institutionalized inclusion and specialization. "Powerful" actors' dominance would not be legitimized without simultaneously possessing these two factors; while the seemingly strong power might not get acceptance simply because the legitimate process cannot depend on power's self-action.
4. The fact that power is accepted as authority is a phase of a process. Acceptable dominance and willing obedience only happen when the power relationship is fluid and it is related to the ever-changing process of the connective system. A long-term view is necessary and in the long run, for the purpose of constructing accepted dominance, static and rigid construction of self-acting power is doomed to failure. No matter how powerful a self-acting power is at one point in time, it is only a temporary phase of an endless process. There is no eternal means of power construction and authority is especially time sensitive.

In sum, connective authority is the authority in which dominance is legitimated and obedience becomes voluntary by a proper and timely construction of the connection to a connective system. The essence of domination and obedience can be formulated as: my acceptance of your power is not because you are powerful as such. Instead, it is because you use your power to connect me and others in the system in a certain way that makes my very existence depend on your existence as such. The type of relationship between you and me and all the others in the contemporary shape constitutes my best interests. The concept "connective authority" has a wide array of implications in international affairs. It can dramatically enhance "hard" power by legitimizing it in a socially acceptable way; it can also transform artificial "soft" power into a deep-rooted social force.

THE WEBERIAN FORMULATION REFRAMED

The Weberian typology—his three ideal types of authority: traditional, charismatic, and legal-rational—is commonly perceived as an exhaustive analysis of the social phenomenon of domination and obedience. For Weber, authority, the legitimized and acceptable power of governance, is no longer centered on a dichotomy of the ruled and the rulers where the two are absolutely separated. He is very insightful in terms of connecting these two sides, although there are limitations when we use this theory to analyze the transformation of power into authority. In his definition of the three ideal types of authority, Max Weber clearly introduces his view. In the description of the "charisma" type, Weber asserts:

> The term charisma shall be understood to refer to an extraordinary quality of a person, regardless of whether this quality is actual, alleged, or presumed. Charismatic authority, hence, shall refer to a rule over men, whether predominantly external or pre-dominantly internal, to which the governed submit because of their belief in the extraordinary quality of the specific person. The magical sorcerer, the prophet, the leader of hunting and booty expeditions, the warrior chieftain, the so-called Caesarist ruler, and under certain conditions, the personal head of a party are such types of rulers for their disciples, followings, enlisted troops, parties, et cetera. The legitimacy of their rule rests on the belief in and the devotion to the extraordinary, which is valued because it goes beyond the normal human qualities, and which was originally valued as supernatural. Charismatic rule is not managed according to general norms, either traditional or rational, but, in principle, according to concrete revelations and inspirations, and in this sense, charismatic authority is irrational.[2]

Here, it seems like "Caesarist" rulers are separated from the common people and they gain their power and authority by their extraordinary capability. However, Weber pointed out that the source of power for charisma to achieve its "extraordinary and supernatural" effects is the successful relatedness of the extraordinary and supernatural individuals to the ordinary folks. In this view, ordinary folks are also connected through their common admiration, worship and devotion to the leader with charisma. Since there is a connection between the extraordinary and the ordinary and among the ordinary folks, the ordinary people are indeed part of the process of constructing the divine power of certain individuals. The interaction is clearly two-sided. Only based on this foundation does the legitimacy of this type of authority emerge.

Understanding international relations using this type of power legitimation clearly highlights an aspect of connective power dynamics. It is only possible for a certain nation to possess charismatic authority when it is regarded by others as a divine place where extraordinary power is amassed and God is with it. Its power would therefore be irrationally legitimized and accepted by the other nations. It is not an easy process but there have been countless efforts toward this direction throughout history across the globe, and a small minority of them indeed succeeded. A nation therefore rises within the framework of the connective web of nations. Although it is still kept as one among many by the connective web, it is the irrational connection that makes it distinctive and extraordinary. However, it has to be clear that this result can only be made possible by connections. Any individual effort to seek power legitimation through creating a sense of awe about the divinity of a specific nation in international relations would be doomed to failure. Sadly, many national leaders, even some thinkers, keep committing this mistake.

As for rational/legal authority, as well as its institutional reflection, the modern bureaucracy, Weber defines it as:

> Submission under legal authority. . . based upon an impersonal bond to the generally defined and functional duty of office. The official duty—like the corresponding right to exercise authority: the jurisdictional competency—is fixed by rationally established norms, by enactments, decrees, and regulations, in such a manner that the legitimacy of the authority becomes the legality of the general rule, which is purposely thought out, enacted, and announced with formal correctness.[3]

This kind of power legitimation is widely used in international politics. As we all well know, the precondition for all legal constructions is based on a pre-assumption: the legal system is abstract and impersonal. It is an "organized and regulated domination" of the "legal persons." While the "legal persons" must be independently rational and act as independent and separated agents for their own interests, their very rationality and interests are constructed through the impersonal constructions of the social connections through the legal system. This is the foundation for all legal deliberations and constructions. We may see clearly that it is impersonalized individuals who face the abstract and rational/legal institution (bureaucracy) as their ruler. The relationship between these two sides is characterized by systematically constructed organizational bonds, which are formal, impersonal and functional. It works as an external force and as an abstract construction to the individuals under its rule. Here, nations can be constructed in a standardized way and transformed into tools of other nations without knowledge of it. The constant efforts of some leading nations to establish rational/legal systems and push for their acceptance across the globe highlight this point. It seems clear that if you want to exercise power over others and make the others accept it, the best and most effective way is to impersonalize yourself and the others and forge an impersonal connection.

Weber's third type, traditional authority, is also based on the notion of connectiveness. According to Weber, "Traditionalism. . . refer(s) to the psychic attitude-set for the habitual workaday and to the belief in the everyday routine as an inviolable norm of conduct. Domination that rests upon this basis, that is, upon piety for what actually, allegedly, or presumably has always existed, will be called traditionalist authority." He continues:

> Patriachalism is by far the most important type of domination, the legitimacy of which rests upon tradition. Partriachalism means the authority of the father, the husband, the senior of the house, the sib elder over the members of the household and sib; the rule of the master and patron over bondsmen, serfs, freed man; of the lord over the domestic servants and household officials; of the prince over house — and court — officials, nobles of office, clients, vassals; of the patrimonial lord and sovereign prince (landesvater) over the subjects.[4]

Here, Weber puts it very clearly that the relationship among different individuals rests upon inter-action. The value system in such a society is not individualistic; that is, people follow the collective norms. The father, the husband, the senior of the house, the sib elders who are playing powerful roles are all propelled by their relationships in the process of obtaining their power in a setting of collective norms. The same holds true for the master and patron when they dominate bondsmen, serfs, or freed men; the lord ruling his domestic servants and household officials; the prince over house- and court-officials, nobles of office, clients, and vassals; the patriamonial lord sovereign prince (Landesvater) over his subjects. In each case, the two opposing sides are very clearly bounded in the power relationship legitimized by externally constructed norms; in this light there are little intrinsic and inseparable relationships. Their interactions and connections are governed by extrinsic collective norms in the form of Durkheimian "mechanic solidarity."

When nations connect to each other in the connective power dynamics, norms play an important role in term of legitimizing power relationships because they are seemingly accepted by each independent player. International laws might be regarded as the condensation of the norms.

Despite its significant potential of application in analyzing global authority systems, the Weberian formulation has serious limitations when it deals with two prevailing situations: the dominance through economic, political or military conquest and the dominance through interdependence.

THE LOGIC OF CONQUEST AND
THE AUTHORITY OF INSTRUMENTATION

"Conquest" is common in international relations. It has been a major theme that has run through the entirety of human history. When we opened a history book, it would be strange if we did not see war and warriors. Although, in the end, the reality might be as Jonathan Schell asserts: the world is unconquerable; so much human energy, talent, time, and so many lives have been spent on the efforts of conquest. Conquest is to defeat and overcome others; it is both an end and a means. In terms of being an end, it satisfies the drive for power, the drive to feel good through domination, the drive to gain self-confidence through others' submission. It is a means because it enables the conqueror to use others as tools to accomplish whatever he wants. Conquest is, therefore, derived from both irrational impulse and rational calculation. It calls for being the strongest carrying a big club; building up overwhelming military power to defeat the enemy and deter everybody else; and then, after "bombing them back to the stone age" and destroying their capability to resist, setting up a rationally designed system—nation building—to make them behave the way we like.

Because of the connective nature of international power dynamics, the logic of conquest generates a "warrior's dilemma." Conquest depends on force. Force can only be effective when it can generate fear. For the conventional enemy in conventional warfare, they fight and kill to live. This is an easy situation. It is possible that they will surrender once their capability of resistance is completely destroyed. However, even in such an easy situation, the "warrior" still faces a dilemma: If conquest is similar to harvest and harvest means to enjoy the fruits the field bears, the most valuable fruit is the people—whether the conquered people will work for the conqueror with their creativity and ingenuity. For this purpose, the warrior has to create the willing compliance of his former enemies beyond generating fear and greed. How is it possible to achieve this goal?

The more difficult situation is when the warrior faces another type of enemy who has no fear. They adhere to the doctrine that "If I cannot kill you, I kill myself, so you'll live miserably." This is a typical terrorist philosophy which posts a difficult situation for the warrior who carries out the logic of conquest.

Another type of dilemma a warrior might face is a partner who is 60% a friend and 40% an enemy. There is no clear-cut black and white; everybody is gray and changing. All of these situations would make the warrior face the difficulty of setting up an award/punishment system based on generating the subjects' greed and fear. The only way to deal with the situations after conquest is to establish instrumental authority.

Instrumental authority can be defined as the following: first, power legitimizes itself through facilitating an effective structure which includes all the significant social forces on the conquered land. Here, it must be clear that the structure must be formed through a natural process in which all the forces naturally grow into their positions. A constant mistake a warrior makes is to force a structure upon the conquered people and cause a mismatch between the real powerful social force in the society and the artificial structure the warrior sets up.

Second, the warrior must strategically position himself in the structure and play a functional role to make the structure work. The major task for the warrior is to transform each party's pursuit of individual interests into part of this structure. Only through this structure and by adhering to relating to each other can they materialize their interests. Here, the warrior's whole thinking cannot be self-interest oriented. It cannot insist on its interests without paying enough attention to the underlying structure of everybody's interests. More importantly, it has to behave as though relationship is more critical than interests. To be more accurate, it has to construct the relationship that can transform the individual pursuit of interests. For this purpose, it itself must be relational and flexible instead of single-mindedly in pursuit its pre-fixed interests.

Third, the most difficult part in terms of setting up instrumental authority is to deal with the forces who have nothing to lose if they fight. If they want to die in order to make your life miserable, your construction of interests through relationship might not work. But, pure relationship without involving considerations of interests will work. The only weapon to deal with people like that is connection. To connect to the network they have connection with and share that connection is the most effective way to subdue these people. For this purpose, the warrior must be able to give up its "either/or" world view. It cannot see the world as either black or white. Connection is paramount. Moral standards and values, as well as material interests, must serve the purpose of connection. It should be clear that connection can change "them" more, although "we" might have to change, too.

This construction is supported by a cognitive institution. The cognitive institution is the benchmark of how smart we are collectively. At the same time, it highlights the limitation of human wisdom at that point in history. But human wisdom does not develop in vacuum. The "collective wisdom" is based on the interaction of the following three major components of human wisdom: rationality, relationality and contextuality. Once we focus on the interaction of these three components of human wisdom, we will get a sense of our cognitive limitations and understand the meaning of instrumental authority.

First of all, if we look at power or authority solely from a pure rational perspective, we can see it is not completely reliable. It is limited in terms of supporting a fully functional organization. As we all know, there are always gaps and loopholes in legal constructions. Rationality can help set up standards and prescribe scripts for our daily activities. But it cannot cover all the ground in our daily organizational life. Our cognitive capability is constrained and framed by certain things and we can only think in a box. If we examine our daily thinking closely, we will discover that we cannot even think consistently. Our interpretations to the happenings around us are constantly self-contradictory. We do not really know our long term interests, let alone consistently fight for them. We have limited capability to receive and process information; we have limited capability to make sense of others. All of these are rooted in our limited rationality. At this point, Max Weber is inadequate. He worshipped human rationality and overlooked the limitations of it. Relationality and contextuality might help us overcome many of these limitations. If we are religious, we might say God is always smarter than we are. However, from the scientific point of view, we know as a fact that to be relational and contextual is smarter than completely relying on individual rationality.

Second, once we are clear about the limitations of our individual rationality, we can know the importance of collective human wisdom. Here I emphasize "collective." For an organization, the key issue should not be single-handedly constructing authority. It should be, in fact, collectively processing the authority system through effective connections. The institutional construction of power and formal authority must go through collective processing, a dynamic process that materializes relationality and contextuality. As a power holder with a purpose of constructing an authority system, we do not want to impose an institution with a formal authority system on the people and hope to use this institutionalized authority to power-over them. We want to connect to them in order to maximize our human resources and stretch our human wisdom to its ultimate limits. Only collective processing can achieve this purpose. Here, weak ties, or social connections, are the essential mechanism. Authority is rooted in intersubjective or collective processes.

Third, collective processing must be based on relationality and contextuality, in addition to rationality. Rationality is a reflection of a sense of control. It is based on a kind of "everything is under control" mentality. It assumes that as long as we can get enough information, we will be able to reach an ideal decision. Therefore, it encourages us to focus on ourselves and try to make ourselves stronger. Relationality, however, is based on recognition of our vulnerability. It means sharing vulnerability in order to achieve mutual empowerment. It attempts to push us to gain strength through sharing our weakness with the people we have relationships with. Mutual empowerment would be a key for relationality. It focuses on "making relationships work" instead of on "making myself stronger." Once the relationship works, we will enable others to do what they otherwise would not be able to do and, in the mean time, they would enable us to do what we otherwise would not be able to do.

Contextuality highlights the fact that we are an aspect of something bigger. We are not only relationally one among many, but also an incomplete one. Without co-existing together with others, we are not able to exist at all. Contextuality highlights a way of thinking that always orients toward actively constructing and actively responding to the surrounding context. Unlike a rationalist way of thinking, which assumes that we know our needs and want and are capable of fulfilling these needs and wants through cost-benefit calculation, contextual thinking does not assume we know the cost-benefit through rational reasoning. Our very needs and wants are fluid and shaped by the context. Only by actively responding to the context can we know and fulfill our needs and wants. If relationality regards other individuals we have relationships with as resources of mutual empowerment, contextuality would regard all those people as the source of collective wisdom.

Here, if we want to solve the warrior's dilemma, we would have to go beyond our rationality and think in a way of relationality and contextuality. All the formal constructions of authority must be centered on connections among different types of people and functional role-playing as an aspect of the system. The Weberian rational/legal authority must work together with instrumental authority, which is based on relationality and contextuality. An authority system needs the rationalized functions of each position and constructs a commanding chain based upon "rationalized" analyses of its function. But it is likely that it would end up playing power for power's sake without fulfilling its true purpose. The construction of a commanding chain must be centered on facilitating connectedness and generate functional role-playing. The concepts of rationality, relationality and contextuality are interdependent.

As a warrior trying to fulfill the purpose of conquest, no matter how s/he organizes the system, s/he must make the structure facilitate her/his subordinates' sense of connection and make her/himself play a central role in the structure. The sense of connectedness must be "built- in" to the structure. To facilitate people's sense of connection is more important than the internal logic of task accomplishment. This whole argument is based on the understanding of the limits of human rationality. We might think we are logical in terms of accomplishing our tasks; we might think we are doing our best to reach a solution for certain situations. But we might produce the opposite effect as the warrior's dilemma would indicate. What should we do? We can only maximize our limited rationality by maximizing relationality and contextuality. We therefore do not possess the rational capability to construct a power-over structure to enforce everything from the top down. An instrumental authority is essentially a system of empowerment which enables people under it to do something constructive they otherwise would not be able to do. For this purpose, conquest must not be for us only. It must be both for them and for us in the first place. Consequently, the warrior would be eventually ready to give up some of the control and facilitate more power centers. In sum, the only precondition for the warrior to resolve the warrior dilemma is to transform conquest power into instrumental authority. Conquest without authority of instrumentation is doomed to failure.

A good example can be illustrated through the comparison between multinational corporations and global corporations. These two business models and their different levels of success can help us see the significance of the authority of instrumentation and the problems without it. Both multinational and global corporations are huge businesses that operate in many countries. However, the former refers to those businesses that do not integrate the local elements of human resources, production, marketing and service forces while the latter refers to those that fully utilize and integrate the local elements. As Kenichi Ohmae mentioned in his influential book, *Borderless World: Power and Strategy in the Interlinked Economy*,[5] Multi-national corporations are classic models of imperialism in the area of business management. They develop business in many countries by cloning themselves and implanting the cloned model in other countries. The corporate headquarters keeps its purity in terms of personnel and corporate culture and enforces this purity throughout the corporation across the globe. The basic assumption underlying this practice is that the headquarters assumes it knows everything and it can exert effective control throughout the corporation. But the problem is that it cannot possibly know everything and it does not have the resources to control everything. So wherever there is a problem, it has to assemble the best management team the corporation can possibly come up with and send it to the troubled branch—the baby company. Even this dream team composed of "stars" in the corporation can constantly encounter insurmountable difficulties because they, in fact, know little about the local issues. In the contemporary business world, this model is considered a failed one because it is still bounded by national boundaries and hence has limited capability to expand and take root globally.

However, the global corporation model is considered true business without boundaries. Within the corporation, it is a borderless world. The corporation incorporates all the local elements in its branches and relinquishes control of the local business to the local branches. On the other hand, its headquarters is filled with people from all over the world. This organizational principle makes it possible for it to "think globally while acting locally"—a winning strategy in global competition. The fundamental assumption is clear: the headquarters does not assume it knows everything and does not try to control everything. It therefore developed a good organization based on a sound cognitive pillar, besides the legal and normative ones. The highest level of authority it exercises is clearly instrumental—through playing its necessary functions and occupying central positions in the business operations to exercise power and dominance.

The cognitive assumption and actual organization of the War on Iraq resembles the multinational corporation model. The US government failed to ask and answer a key question: do we have sufficient connections to the local elites in order to guarantee local support in the post-war reconstruction? Since the US launched the war without sufficient power, as well as intention, to utilize the local elements to manage the post-war situation, it has had to send in the best management team composed of the best military, economic and political leaders the US can come up with to Iraq to deal with the crisis. However, regardless of how excellent this team is, it cannot take root in Iraqi society. Without the sufficient support from the local society through the local elites, the mission can never be accomplished. Here we see the limitations of liberal democracy in terms of bestowing genuine authority onto the people who won the election. Unlike in the mature democratic society where the election symbolizes, more or less, the deep-rooted social connections between the elected and the electorate, the system of representative democracy is imposed from outside the society in Iraq. The elected people are not necessarily the most connected people in the society and therefore their real power is limited. This group of people, no matter how motivated they are to be part of the US occupation system, cannot work as effectively as those local elements working in a global corporation. Furthermore, a political situation is much more complicated than a business one. A business organization can simply incorporate the people who are capable of running the business without having to worry about the consequence of the exclusion of other social elements. The political organization must deal with all the powerful social elements in the local society at the same time. Therefore, besides the authority of instrumentation, it has to depend on another type of authority, the authority of inclusion, which is the topic of next section.

THE LOGIC OF INTERDEPENDENCE
AND THE AUTHORITY OF INCLUSION

In international relations, the logic of interdependence is much more appealing than the logic of conquest. In fact, it is based on a liberal formula:

economic interdependence through market economy + international institutions + democratic nation-state system = peace and prosperity of the international system

Under this logic, market mechanisms are the foundations of the international system while nation-states are the unit of action. To make the market mechanisms work smoothly, a domestic democratic system, in a sense of representative democracy, is necessary. In the realm beyond nation-states, the system relies on international institutions. International cooperation is therefore possible without a political authority in the modern international system.[6] The key is interdependence, but it is in the context of the following two facts. The first fact is that all the international institutions are weak and that it is close to impossible to establish strong ones. Therefore, nation-states act as separated action units without a world government to maintain order and keep justice. The second fact is that international interdependence is based on the short-term exchange of interests of the nation-states. Therefore, transactional gains in the forms of strategic interests or material profits are regarded as paramount.

Therefore, it would have to deal with a merchant's dilemma: doing business with everyone or with gentlemen only? It is clear that the possibility of equal exchange and the existence of independent and dependable units are the preconditions for interdependence. If some units are not reliable, or they do not possess equal capability and resource to be dependable in an exchange relationship, it will be impossible for an interdependent relationship to develop. The system of interdependence is therefore highly exclusive—it only includes independent units that are strong and resourceful enough to be dependable. The multi-polar power system it derived is not able to empower the less powerful. It automatically becomes a system of "rule of many by the few." As a consequence, it creates enmity between those system insiders and those who are excluded. High levels of alienation and antagonism naturally follow.

Here we might need to discuss the notion of "democratic peace." It is a fact that democratic nation-states are rarely at war with each other. For the purpose of establishing the connection between domestic political systems to international order, scholars in the field of international studies have provided rich interpretations on this issue.[7] But I would say that although domestic democratic politics and international peace are highly correlated, the relationship between them is a correlation instead of a causation. The real causal factor that makes international peace happen is international interdependence. The logic is based on the fundamental sociological proposition: a group can only be understood on the group level—it can never be understood on the individual level based on examining its individual members. 1+1 in a group setting never equals 2. It is always possible that a group of saints might still fight against each other over some "lofty" issues; the "my way or the highway" philosophy applies to everyone in a group setting. Benevolent nations have interests and will the same as evil empire; popular favor, as it is often manipulated by the powerful people in the democratic nation-states, is equally forceful to push a nation into war. Same as individuals, nation-states have the potential to be both peaceful and warlike and it all depends on the international dynamics to bring either side out. The international dynamic behind democratic peace is the authority of inclusion. If we observe carefully, a clear pattern emerges: it is the international mechanism of inclusion based on equal exchange and mutual dependency that causes democratic states to co-exist peacefully. These peacefully co-existing nation-states not only have democratic political system, but also operate under market economies with rich economic resources and strong productivity to conduct equal exchange. They are the "gentlemen" of the rich country's club. Hence, the drive to do business with gentlemen inside the club that keeps them together peacefully. The shared democratic political system, with its power to produce trust, transparency, and mutual understanding is, of course, one of the major factors. But it only works under the international mechanism of inclusion. The conclusion is hence clear: it is the system of inclusion that produces peace; only when a nation-state is smoothly included in the international system can it be a peaceful partner.

However, while the mechanism of inclusion produces peace among the Western industrialized nations, it has, at the same time, created a system of exclusion—it automatically excludes other nations that are not capable of being equal partners. As it is easy to understand, it is not easy to do business with someone who is different from us and who also has little to offer. It is not simply because these nation-states are not democratic. Their undemocratic political systems are only a surface reflection about their overall incapability of being equal partners to be included in the club. They are not dependable in an interdependence system. The merchant's dilemma is clear here: how can we develop an interdependent relationship with the people/nations that are not dependable? While inclusion creates peace, exclusion produces potential trouble-makers to the insiders.

The only effective way to minimize the merchant's dilemma is the authority of inclusion. It is based on a fact that all of us are on a life-boat with nowhere to go: we only have limited space to be shared with friends as well as enemies at the same time. Like it or not, we have to stay together forever.

In an uncomfortable situation like this, the best strategy would be to have a long-term view with the possibility of sacrificing immediate interests. A necessary mentality would have to focus on the good and tolerate all the imperfections—no matter how bad they are. The most effective survivors are those who seek to change "them" and "us" in a dynamic process of developing relationships and make efforts to construct an inclusive, but hierarchical, system. In this system, a relational web works as the fundamental structure of world order. Relationship is paramount and national interests are secondary. In fact, there is no fixed and predetermined national interest or national identity without referring it to the specific relationships constructed by the nation-states involved. There is no space to be too individualistic. Relationship is more valuable than specific interest. The approach "my way or the highway" is doomed to be punished by the connective power dynamics. The fact is that the inescapable connections facilitate a hierarchical system that enables the well connected nation-states to possess stronger power over the less connected ones. Authority is therefore derived from the quality and quantity of connections. The more connected nation-states are the more dynamic forces that shape the world order. In the process of pushing the gradual improvement of their positions, connectedness in a social sense bestows the global leadership to those that can better exercise the authority of inclusion.

Only through "sailing with everybody" and including all the parties that can exercise some power on the global issues, can the leading nation-state gain access and acceptance of those who are not dependable and push these undependable nation-states to be more dependable in an interdependent system. The most salient and recent example might be the six-party talks in dealing with North Korea.

According to the logic of interdependence, it is a sure thing that North Korea is not dependable. The United States, as well as many other nation-states, feels highly uncomfortable sailing with it and including it in the international interdependent system. However, North Korea is not too remote to be ignored. It is not easy to insulate it; it is not productive to exclude it. On the contrary, it is the authority of inclusion that made North Korea do something it otherwise would not do—to dismantle its nuclear facilities and submit to international examination.

Iran is not a far away place either. The international society cannot afford to ignore it and exclude it and it cannot be conquered. On the surface, we see the mechanism of interdependence would not work because Iran is not dependable. However, the connective approach can offer a solution: establish/normalize a relationship first; change it later—and be ready to be changed; steadily construct and firmly pursue a flexible national interest through a gradual and dynamic process.

The authority of inclusion has two sides: the formal and the informal. The formal side is the legal and normative construction of the international system that fully includes all nation-states. The United Nations is a good existing forum but its lack of leadership is obvious. The key issue is social embeddedness. The formal side will not work if it is not embedded in the informal side.

The informal side is international connections which include all the relevant parties. We trust the power of social connectedness in international interactions. The more connected a nation-state is, the better and more responsible it will be. The connective power dynamics is clearly highlighted here: there is a close association between "Doing with" and "Doing for"—joining and doing good are very closely related. The more a nation is involved and included, the more altruistic behavior it tends to display. Altruistic behaviors only happen when nations are together. Who among us are most generous with our toil and treasure? The most connected. Connectedness is the most consistent predictor. The authority of inclusion, as well as the collective power underneath it, is very powerful in terms of transforming an individual nation's beliefs, its financial capital and its military might for a good purpose. It is potentially possible that simply being asked in a friendly manner might be the sole reason for a nation's leaders to decide to do something good. It is always true that connectedness shapes the habits of the human heart.

MODIFICATION OF THE WEBERIAN TYPOLOGY[8]

The two types of authority we just discussed differ from Weber's three ideal types in that they take the connective "system" where everyone is connected to everyone else, rather than the individual social entity, as the basic unit of analysis. Therefore, they are regarded on a higher level. They share with the idea of charismatic authority a focus on the distinctive role of strong persons or nations in the authority structure, and share the premise that these dominant social entities may shape the direction of social change. But, in addition to the hero worship of ordinary people and the personal attractiveness of charisma, authorities of instrumentation and inclusion rely on a stable and routinized web of connective ties which shape the interests and capability of every individual social "entity," regardless of whether it is strong or weak. This construction departs from the charismatic one in two crucial respects.

First, these two types of authority are indeed authoritarian in nature, in that they support the role of the strong in controlling the weak and securing obedience. At the same time, however, power here is web-based. Hero worship is rare and an individual entity's charismatic attractiveness is very limited.

They highlight the notion that the powerful get their power from the web of connective ties as a whole. Therefore, there is a possibility of positive incentives for the weaker partners to participate, because if there is a power over them, it is a web-based power which gains its power through its role and position in the web and they, the weak social "entities," nonetheless, are members of the web. Central to these two types of authority is the notion that the connection between the stronger and weaker parties is mutually stimulated in the web. Sharing vulnerability plays a critical part in the process of mutuality. They therefore affirm the possibility of the extraordinary but do not entertain the idea of the "divine power" of the charismatic figure; they fundamentally differ from the notion of individualistic charismatic power.

Second, the interconnected and undetachable social and economic institutions that comprise the web of connective ties serve as the venue for strengthening and deepening the inseparability of the system as a whole. Because of these institutional constructions, instrumental and inclusive authorities are a routinized rational relationship. It posits a rich subculture of instrumental and rational connections through which individual social "entities" directly and indirectly circumvent formal regulations to obtain the recognized status in the connective web. They do not share the quality of irrationality with charismatic authority; all activities are carefully calculated by each individual social entity as an "aspect" of the connective system.

Authority of instrumentation and authority of inclusion share with the traditional one the collective social ties that play an important role in the formation of social structure. Yet, they depart from the "traditional type" of authority in four fundamental ways.

First, as we have noted above, ties among social entities in these two types of authority are conceived as an intrinsic part of each individual social "entity," helping to shape its sense of self, its interests and its capability, rather than external to it. Because of this intrinsic nature, the connective ties are not an external means to connect separated and clearly bounded individual social "entities." They are intrinsic parts of the web.

Second, ties among social "entities" are rather more indirect compared to the face to face direct contact present in the traditional type of authority. These two types of authority are exercised within concentric circles of web which may stretch from direct ties to a potentially unlimited web of connective ties.

Third, these two types of authority do not rely too much on traditional norms or values to maintain their power. They are an informally and formally institutionalized web which is not only deeply rooted in individual social entities' "relational selves," but also compatible with the current and rationally constructed organizational structure in which people within each social "entity" make their livings. The rich subculture through which they exist is, rather, independent from the traditional norms and values of the past.

Fourth, under these two types of authority, domination and obedience rest upon naturally formed social relationships. In addition, as the "web" overlaps with existing socio-economic structures in which each social "entity" participates, domination and obedience are both institutional and relational; both rational and emotional; and both functional and contextual. In all of this, there is nothing arbitrary; everything is based upon a system, and is framed by rationally established institutional norms. Tradition plays only a minor role here.

Authority of instrumentation and authority of inclusion share with Weber's rational-legal type a rational deliberation that forms the base for its operationalization. But, their root of legitimacy goes beyond the impersonal bond of the generally defined functional "duties of office." They therefore depart from the rational-legal type in a crucial way. In addition to the impersonal mobilization and bureaucratic atomization, instrumental and inclusive authorities stress collectively established and organized particularism. They include the bureaucratic organization as the basic unit of political and economic connection, or as the basic element of social structure. They also emphasize networks which are formed from the rational choices of separated individual social entities. In addition, the web of connective ties forms the intrinsic nature of sense of selves of all social "entities;" the socially developed web of connective ties is therefore seen as the basic unit of organizational behavior.[9]

Inseparable individual social "entities" are joined within the web of direct and indirect ties which are supported by the bureaucracy, as well as instrumental-personal ties independent from the legal-rational bureaucracy's control. There is an institutionalized and inseparable interconnection between the connective web and individual social "entities." Social "entities" are bound together by the institutionalized or social web of connective ties. This web is invisible and omnipresent, with a possibility of lasting through a life-time in a forever together community. Although individual social 'entities" are rational within the web of transactional ties, they have very limited space to exercise their rational choice to choose among the ties in the web to which they would have to belong. It is this socially bounded relational web that distinguishes instrumental and inclusive authorities from the rational-legal type. The web is held together by an intrinsic sense of belonging to the connective social ties and these two types of authority are embedded in the web.

In sum, the authority of instrumentation and the authority of inclusion are types of authority in which power is legitimized by its unitary link of individual social "aspects" to the web of connective ties on both internal and external, institutional and social levels. They go beyond the Weberian three types: it is not a power legitimized by personal supernatural attractiveness;

not by traditional norms; and not by rational-legal constructions. I believe that these two types of authority should be properly considered as the additional types on a higher level above the other three Weberian "types," i.e., traditional, charismatic and legal-rational.

Of course, these two types of authority do not work alone. They work simultaneously and together with and through the other three types. Therefore, we should consider all of them when we use the ideal types of authority as an analytical tool to understand global power dynamics. As Weber himself noted:

> Only a systematic presentation could demonstrate how far the distinctions and terminology chosen here are expedient. Here we may emphasize merely that by approaching in this way, we do not claim to use the only possible approach nor do we claim that all empirical structures of domination much correspond to one of these "pure" types. On the contrary, the great majority of empirical cases represent a combination or a state of transition among several such pure types.[10]

The formulation of authority of instrumentation and authority of inclusion appears to have validity both deductively (in that Weber's initial typology of authority is not exhaustive) and inductively (in the sense that it highlights the legitimacy of the emerging forms of connective power dynamics). In daily international interactions, these types of authority legitimize the connective power dynamics in concrete ways. We would regard them as the basic types of authority: charismatic authority, traditional authority, rational/legal authority, and on a higher level, instrumental authority and inclusive authority. All these five types of authority reveal the most fundamental logics of social relations.

NOTES

1. Max Weber, *From Max Weber: essays in sociology*, Hans H. Gerth and C. Wright Mills, eds. (paperback edition, New York: Oxford University Press, 1958): 78.
2. Max Weber, 295–296.
3. Max Weber, 299.
4. Max Weber, 296
5. Kenichi Ohmae, *Borderless World: power and strategy in the interlinked economy,* (revised edition, New York: HarperBusiness, 1999).
6. For detailed description about the liberal construction of the international logic,see Robert O. Keohane, *After Hegemony: Cooperation and Discord in the World Political Economy* (Princeton, NJ: Princeton University Press, 1984); Robert O. Keohane, "Theory of World Politics: Structural Realism and Beyond," in Ada W. Finifter, ed. *Political Science: The State of the Discipline* (Washington, D.C.: American Polit-

ical Science Association, 1983): 503–540; Kenneth A. Oye, ed. *Cooperation under Anarchy* (Princeton, NJ: Princeton University Press, 1985).

7. There are several different accounts of the logic behind the democratic peace argument. For liberal ideas, see Bruce Russett, *Grasping the Democratic Peace* (Princeton: Princeton University Press, 1993); James Ray, *Democracy and International Conflict,* (Columbia: University of South Carolina Press, 1995); For institutions that make up democracy, see Kurt Gaubatz, "Democratic States and the Commitment in International Relations," *International Organization* 50: 1 (1996): 109–39; Brett Ashley Leeds, "Democratic Political Institutions, Credible Commitments, and International Cooperation," *American Journal of Political Science* 43: 4 (1999): 979–1002; Charles Lipson, *Reliable Partners* (Princeton: Princeton University Press, 2003); For arguments that embrace both theoretical orientations, see Michael Doyle, "Liberalism and World Peace," *American Political Science Review* 80: 4 (1986): 1151–69; John Owen, "How Liberalism Produces the Democratic Peace," *International Security,* 19: 2 (1994): 87–125.

8. This section is based on one of my term papers for an independent study with Dr. Paul S. Gray in Boston College in 1995. I would like to express my deep gratitude to Dr. Gray for his spiritual encouragement, theoretical guidance, and editing efforts.

9. Here, I am indebted to some of the conceptualization in Andrew Walder's *Communist Neo-Traditionalism* (Walder: 1986, Berkeley, CA: University of California Press, 1986): 5–14. The major departure of my theoretical assumption from his is that how much rational choice an individual can exercise in terms of choosing the web he or she wants to belong to. Rather than treating rational individual units of action or rationally formed networks as basic units of analysis, I regard the life-time bounded "web" of ties as an inseparable unit and treat it as the unit of analysis.

10. Max Weber, 299-300.

Chapter Four

Connective Democracy
and Global Governance

A GOVERNMENT OR A GOVERNANCE SYSTEM-IN-BEING?

World Government

This book sets out to answer three fundamental questions about global governance: Is international society governable? Do we have a system of global governance? If we do, what is it? The book purports to provide a definitive answer to these questions: yes, the international society is governable and the system of governance is based upon social dynamics (termed connective power dynamics) through a legitimized system called connective authority. The basic idea is that togetherness is the main characteristic of global order and it can make individual nation-states be good. You do not have to hold a pessimistic view about individuals and society if you are a realist.

Hans J. Morgenthau in his classic book, *Politics among Nations: the Strength for Power and Peace,* expresses a common view on the issue of a world government:

> There is no shirking the conclusion that international peace cannot be permanent without a world state and that a world state cannot be established under the present moral, social, and political conditions of the world. In the light of what has been said thus far in this book, there is also no shirking the further conclusion that in no period of modern history was civilization more in need of permanent peace and, hence, of a world state, and that in no period of modern history were the moral, social and political conditions of the world less favorable for the establishment of a world state. There is, finally, no shirking the conclusion that, as there can be no state without a society wiling and able to support it, there can be no world state without a world community willing and able to support it.[1]

The idea is clear here: we need a world state but we are not able to have one. The reason for this situation is also clear: we do not have a world community that is willing and able to support a world government. But from the connectivist perspective, this assertion needs further discussion because of the following points.

World Community

My definition of "world community" is different from Morgenthau's. According to him, a world community mirrors a nation and should possess the major characteristics of a nation. As he puts it,

> There does not exist a supranational society that comprises all individual members of all nations and, hence, is identical with humanity politically organized. The most extensive society in which most men live and act in our times is the national society. The nation is, as we have seen, the recipient of man's highest secular loyalties. Beyond it there are other nations, but no community for which man would be willing to act regardless of what he understands the interests of his own nation to be.[2]

But my understanding is that the global village IS a world community. It is a community based on a simple fact: we are together anyway, regardless of whether we accept it or not. We do not have the luxury of selectively detaching from someone and intentionally getting involved with someone else. On the one hand, the logic of togetherness produces dynamics of empowerment that enable members of the village to do the things they otherwise would not be able to do. Under the circumstances when we are instruments to each other and dependent on each other, we change each other for better. On the other hand, we keep each other hostage in one way or another. To a large extent, even the most powerful member cannot take action to hurt the weakest member based on a single-mindedly constructed national interest without having to endure some painful consequences. People the world over are empowered by their national identities, cultural heritages, and human capital through knowledge possession. They are even more empowered by their connections to the other members of the village. The connection is manifested by economic exchange, by the sense of justice as it is revealed through public opinion, and by international institutions. But more importantly, it is manifested by the knowledge about each other's vulnerability, the ever progressing technological advancements that enable a "democratization of the means of mass destruction," including the fundamentally uncontrollable proliferation of deadly weapons, and the fundamental dependency of national economies on resources that are beyond national control.

Because of this reality, it would be very difficult to mobilize citizens in each individual nation to participate in a deadly war without compelling reasons. It would be harder and harder to answer the question: why do we have to fight by risking so much while we can give up some and gain even more? How large a proportion of the citizenry can be convinced or compelled to fight with the enemy while the enemy can potentially be thirty or forty percent friend?

According to Morgenthau, the readiness to resort to violence by all kinds of social groups is the major dynamic that drives the division that undermines the unity of a community. As he says: "The history of national societies shows that no political, religious, economic, or regional group has been able to withstand for long the temptation to advance its claims by violent means if it thought it could do so without too great a risk."[3] It is true that human beings will take short-cuts if they can do so. But violence is a short-cut for people to advance their interests only if the resistance is minimum. In a global village, as we discussed above, we have developed into a world community that will generate large enough resistance, and therefore risk, for violence.

Conditions of Peace and Effective Global Governance

In terms of the conditions of peace and effective global governance, I agree with Morgenthau's assertion about the three conditions that make domestic peace possible: "overwhelming force, suprasectional loyalties, and expectation of justice."[4] A national governance system is effective only when it fulfills all these conditions. But I do not agree that these conditions are absent on the international scene and that there is no possibility that a global governance system cannot play these functions.

My key argument is that unlike a national government which is a government-in-shape, a global governance system is a system-in-being led by most connected nation-state(s). A national government is based on a fixed formal structure whereas the global governance system is a flexible structure based on relational and functional connections among nations. It is a system by all and for all; its foundation is the inclusive connections and its strategic and inviolable instruments are the nation-state(s) that plays leadership role.

It is true that national government monopolizes the use of force and it possesses overwhelming force against violence among different social groups within the nation. But on the international scene, there is always a possibility that the global leader(s) is capable of amassing overwhelming force against some individual nation-states. The two most recent events that can highlight this point are the first Gulf War and the War on Serbia over Kosovo; both of them were in 1990 when the United States played a functional and relational role that generated overwhelming international force against a transgressor each time. It is clear that an effective global leader can amass sufficient force against any transgressor without a world state as the agent. The result is just as the national government has been playing all along: the very existence, in the hands of the global leader(s) and their allies, of an overwhelming force, "ready to intervene, in case of need," deters any possible disturbances of international peace. "The very fact of its existence makes it unnecessary for the compulsory organization of society to act."[5]

Also, national borders are not necessarily the absolute boundaries of people's loyalties. Just like the situation in the domestic scene, people's interests can be embedded within the densely woven fabric of the international community. The pluralist and overlapping sectional loyalties can happen across national borders. People can be both friends and foes at the same time— maybe 50% friends and 50% foes overall and 40% friends economically and 60% foes politically. Everybody cares about stock value once they invest in the stock market, regardless of their national identities and where the stock market is located. Everybody knows that there are no permanent friends and there is no permanent enemy, either, on the international scene. The surface reason is the ever shifting combination of interests among nation-states. The deeper reason is that the people within national borders have already developed the densely woven fabric among themselves across the national borders—they are interdependent to advance their interests and, in the mean time, share vulnerabilities. The "suprasectional loyalties" exist without a world state to define these loyal relationships.

Can citizens in different nations expect justice to be done by a global system-in-being without a world state? The answer is yes: as long as the leading nation-state(s) can be functional and relational in terms of providing instrumental authority and inclusive authority, we can expect justice on the international scene. The reason is simple: justice is less guaranteed by a legal system and more by the leadership's effort to maintain the status quo. Just as Morgenthau indicated, even domestically, we cannot expect a perfectly impartial justice system. All governance systems cannot help but play a role that enforces the status quo. In this sense, international justice is not much different than domestic justice. As Morgenthau says: "Actually, the compulsory organization of society cannot be completely neutral, for, as we have seen, the legal order it enforces is not completely neutral and cannot help favoring the status quo to which it owes its existence. If challenged, the status quo can count upon the support of the compulsory organization of society."[6]

Like the practice on the domestic scene, the global leader(s), together with their allies in the global governance system-in-being, "are strong enough to keep the resentment and disaffection of such small and weak groups from turning openly against the social order." Yet, although the global leader(s) cannot enforce global justice based upon public opinion, election or parliamentary votes, and the judiciary system, they "cannot afford to remain deaf to the claims for justice of large and potentially powerful" nations . . . "without endangering its peace and its very survival as an integrated whole"—exactly as the national government would do to the large and powerful social groups. "It is here that the intricate mechanism of peaceful change comes into play," giving the nations with sufficient power a chance to claim justice.[7]

I am not here to advocate the doctrine of the divisibility of sovereignty because I agree with Morgenthau that "Far from expressing a theoretical truth or reflecting the actuality of political experience, the advice to give up 'a part of national sovereignty' for the sake of the preservation of peace is tantamount to the advice to close one's eyes and dream that one can eat one's cake and have it, too."[8] However, I say there is indeed a world society and an international order which is on a high level and therefore does not conflict with national sovereignty. The ultimate decision making authority is still in the hands of national government but the global leadership constructs a higher order through its functional and relational connections on the global scale.

Form of Global Governance

The form of world governance according to the connectivist view is different from Morgenthau's world government. According to Morgenthau, a world government

> (1) . . .would give humanity a legal personality that would keep the unity of mankind before its eyes; (2) . . .would create and keep in motion agencies for worldwide social change that might allow all groups of mankind to expect at least some satisfaction for their conflicting claims; (3) . . . would establish enforcement agencies that would meet any threat to the peace with overwhelming strength.[9]

Clearly, Morgenthau's model of world government mirrors the model of a national government. While this form of a world government is too remote to reach, there is still a high possibility of establishing a global governance system.

Obviously, it is impossible for the global governance system to be based on representative democracy. Majority rule would not be acceptable to the powerful minority. It would be impossible to develop a parliament fairly representing such peoples of different faith, loyalties, and perceived interests as the Americans, the Chinese, the Indians, and the Russians and make them into an operating whole. However, it is possible that the constituent groups of a global village might willingly or unwillingly submit to a connective web of international ties with powerful leader(s) and their allies enforcing the decisions. A global governance system thus constitutes the functionally and relationally connected web of all members of the global village. It is a hierarchical web with a legal system and international organizations as supplemental agencies. It is not based on moral or political consensus; it is not based on common political or economic interests either. Its foundation is the functional and relational connections between or among nations with authority of instrumentation and authority of inclusion as its cornerstone. In sum, it is a system-in-being.

The formation of this global governance system is a 3-D model. It is driven by the global leader(s) to form vertical connections between them and the second tiered nation-states and through empowering them, to reach other nation-states. However, it is also horizontal. There are dynamic connections among nation-states in each tier that enable them play their functional roles in the system. In this way, a world order is established and the threat and the actuality of war would therefore be minimized.

The very essence of this system is democratic. It is consistent with the essence of democratic governance—a democracy among the 192 nation-states within the global village. It is an inclusive system by all and for all. Without the democratic process, the system would not be functional. However, it is not democracy as we know it. It represents a new type of democracy, which is termed "connective democracy."

THE ESSENCE OF DEMOCRACY
AND SOME UNRESOLVED ISSUE

The core meaning of democracy seems clear: it means popular power—people as the ultimate political authority. For a long period in history, this notion was not acceptable to many who regarded themselves as "above" the people. As C. B. Macpherson puts it,

> Democracy used to be a bad word. Everybody who was anybody knew that democracy, in its original sense of rule by the people or government in accordance with the will of the bulk of the people, would be a bad thing—fatal to individual freedom and to all the graces of civilized living. That was the position taken by pretty nearly all men of intelligence from the earliest historical times down to about a hundred years ago. Then, within fifty years, democracy became a good thing.[10]

Since "democracy" has become fashionable, the word has been abused or misused by many people with different views and practices. However, we might ask how powerful "the people" have become in comparison to the ones "above" them in a process that transformed the notion of democracy from a bad word to a good one? Have we really developed into a society that is equal enough so those people who are "above" ordinary are no longer able to denounce democracy as an ideal? Have these "above the ordinary" people really disappeared as a factor that distorts the democratic practice? The reality is just the opposite. Those who think themselves "above" the people are still there and alive and well. They are still powerful and "above" the people. Therefore, to understand the relationship between them and the ordinary people will become critical for us to understand the fundamental power dynamics in the democratic political system. The key questions are as follows: where are those people who were "above" the ordinary people? Why did they accept the notion of democracy? If we do not question their motives and how sincere they are, we have to at least know, in reality, how they position themselves so that they can accommodate the popular sovereignty.

In the Cold War era, because of the threat posed by Communism and the Soviet Union, democracy is a way of life we, "the free world," fought to defend. We did not need to think deeply about the detail, the strength and weakness, of our current "democratic" political system. We automatically regarded it as perfect and worthwhile of our efforts to fight for it. Yet, when the Cold War was over, it may have been time for us to move away from the mood of self-congratulation and begin to raise some healthy doubts about the effectiveness of our democratic system as we knew it. Since democracy is the only legitimate form of governance in the world, we need to be clearer than we were before about what the term really means. Otherwise, we might end up promoting something we do not really understand.

To begin with, we know the fact that there is no clear and definitive definition of "democracy," a term with no precise and agreed upon meaning. If we trace back its history, the phenomenon is even more salient. The commonsensical notions are many. We might only need to discuss a few we commonly assume as given.

The first: If a government is elected by the voters of the people, it is democracy. Historically, Hitler was elected fair and square into the Chancellorship; can we say the Third Reich was a democracy? Today, most Iranian high ranking state officials, including its president, are elected by the people; is Iran a democratic country? Hamas was elected to the leadership position of Palestine; why don't we accept it as a democratic regime and provide moral support for it?

The second: If a country's political system is free, it is a democracy. Freedom means to be without fear in the political process. Here it commonly means free speech, freedom of assembly, freedom of beliefs, and, most importantly, freedom of choosing government. But what do we mean by "freedom" exactly? Free from fear of what? Can any nation-state survive without extensive rules and regulations to put a limit on the freedoms listed above? Can any nation-state survive without imposing patriotic language for people to use, official rituals for people to perform, government sponsored organizations to channel people's assemblage, and rules to guide people when they "freely" choose government, which naturally put some social groups in an advantageous position while placing others in disadvantageous positions? As Rousseau mentioned: "How can a man be at once free and forced to conform to wills which are not his own? How can the opposing minority be both free and subject to laws to which they have not consented?"[11]

The third: Democratic government as a whole is by the people; it is at least by the representative of the majority of the people, if not all the people. And government officials as individuals are regarded as elected representatives of the people; they are supposed to be the agents of the people who elected them. How true is this assertion? How many American presidents and their administrations were elected by the majority of the American people? Let us forget about the Presidents before 1920 when the 19th Constitutional Amendment was passed and women got the right to vote. The two most recent Presidents, George W. Bush and Bill Clinton, were both elected by a minority of people. Maybe a better question is: How possible is this "by the people" assertion? People are divided; some of them go to vote, many of them do not. Even the people who show up at the voting booths are also divided if they have genuine choices. If the elected officials are truly the agents of the people who elected them, they can only be the representatives of a minority.

Apparently, most theorists and politicians are against simple majority rule. Their rationale is sound and clear. But if a democratic government is not a representative of the majority, what can it be? Can we say a democratic government is a government for the people? If so, the Iranian government can also claim it is for the people and a very large proportion of the Iranian people would agree. A government "for the people" does not have to be "democratic" as the common conception would regard it to be. If popular support is the indicator of "for the people," we can see the Nazi regime enjoyed popular support for a long time before it faded and the reason for the fading popular support was not because it was not democratic, it was because of Hitler's failed attempts in foreign warfare.

There are some key dilemmas for a democratic political system. The first and most critical is the issue of "general will." As Rousseau insightfully pointed out, "the will of all" often diverges from "the general will." Even when we reach the very rare unanimity, it still cannot guarantee that what we want as individuals is exactly the same as what we want as a community. This

dilemma is rooted in dichotomous thinking: the community is either a sum to-
tal of individuals or an abstract entity beyond all individuals. The liberal democratic theorists insist on the former and regard individual freedom, pluralism, and tolerance of diversity as the hallmark of democracy. Rousseau would
regard unity as the fundamental element of a democracy and insists that "sectional associations" harmful to democracy and the community as a whole. To
accuse Rousseau of being "totalitarian" has simplified the issue. Clearly, in a
democratic world as it is depicted by the liberals, the only possibility is majority rule. But there is a fundamental conflict between individual freedom
and rule by majority groups.

Another key issue is the issue of special interests and the uneven contest
among social groups with different amounts of power. It is clear that not all
interests are automatically legitimate and it is not possible to reach a compromise in all situations. In a representative democracy, it is usually the best-
organized and best-funded groups that prevail. The interests of the people
therefore turn into the interests of the special interest groups that are powerful enough to exert their influence on the political process. The government
is accountable and representative to these groups only. These groups certainly
include large segments of the people in general. But in terms of any specific
issue, it is the small minority that determine the outcome of the democratic
process of the whole. This is a fundamental violation of the democratic principle. Interest group politics have hollowed the principle of majority rule.
Since it is impossible to equalize the power each social group possesses, no
matter how hard the government tries to balance, it would be impossible to
minimize the impact of inequality and effectively address the issue of social
injustice. A direct and clear consequence of this practice is the alienation of
the groups of people who have little chance to win the interest groups' power
contest. They would find that it is hard to trust the democratic system and it
is not worthwhile to support the democratic system. It is clear that under the
circumstance of inequality in terms of wealth and power, as long as the
process is interest-based, the democratic principle is not workable in a representative system.

Furthermore, in a society of inequality, the government is not sovereign
over all aspects of the society. In fact, its power is limited, especially in the
area of economy. In a capitalist society, capital investment is the foundation
of the survival of the society in general. Therefore, the people who possess
capital are naturally in dominant positions. They do not even need to do much
in the political process—the mere fact that they possess the capital, therefore,
the power to make huge differences on so many people's lives would be
enough to force the elected officials to bow to their wishes. It would be an illusion to see all interest groups as competing with each other on a roughly

equal basis and the government in a position to balance out these interests and safeguard social justice. On the contrary, the political landscape is largely a reflection of the economic landscape. In the field of economy, ordinary people are regarded as "human capital" possessed and used by financial capital. Their value depends on how useful they are to the profit-seeking capitalist organizational machine. The huge contradiction between economic inequality and political equality makes the claim that a democratic system is grounded on the combination or balance of various special interest groups merely empty talk. Without the backing of real power, the slogan "one person one vote" has become trivial and irrelevant. The reason is clear: without equality of access to the political system, especially to the powerful people in the system, ordinary people would not have equal opportunity to influence the government. In sum, if it is impossible to equalize economic power among the people, the democratic ideal in an interest-based democratic system is doomed to failure.

Another dilemma for representative democracy is the very term "representative." To a certain degree, D. H. Lawrence's indignant question is legitimate: "who can represent me? I am myself. I don't intend anybody to represent me."[12] Indeed, representation is impossible from the individualistic perspective. It is impossible for anyone to fully understand someone else, speak for him or her without any deviation from the words and accents of he or she would use, and act in a given situation exactly the same way as he or she would act. People even constantly misrepresent themselves, let alone trust in others to represent them. How is it possible that representatives would represent the society as a whole as Burke argued or as Rousseau insisted? In reality, in a representative democracy, the ordinary people have strikingly little control over what their representatives actually do in their names, besides the superficial election. Representatives rarely "represent" their constituents. They make their own judgments and decide the policy issues based on the evaluations they make about the situations. More often than not, it is the representatives who shape the opinion of their constituents instead of vice versa. The key issue is still the ever existing power imbalance. Once one becomes a representative, s/he would become more powerful and resourceful than her/his constituents. A natural drive for power, according to Nan Lin's social capital theory, is to make homophilous connections with the people who have similar power and resources in order to maintain the power and heterphilous connections with the people who are more powerful and resourceful in order to gain more power.[13] Since election is superficial and interest group politics are more fundamental in a representative democracy, the system would only discourage the connections between the representatives and the people who elected them to be their representatives.

Some people might argue that modern technology has made it possible for direct democracy in a large and diverse society. But what does "direct" mean, exactly? The example they give is the Athenian system and referendum. For both of them, we can see the manipulation of the average people by the powerful. In 1992 presidential election, candidate Ross Perot proposed a direct democratic form characterized as the "electronic town hall meeting." The Perot-style electronic town hall is a kind of plebiscitary democracy which is depended on modern technology. But modern technology itself is a high divisive factor. It inevitably excludes a large proportion of the people who cannot afford the access to the modern high tech, who are careless about high tech, who lack the cultural habit to learn high tech. Also, direct ballot initiative is very expensive, not only for the organizers, but also for the participants. It is expensive not only in financial terms—it is certainly a key factor—but also in cultural and social terms. The people who are financially worry free, who are culturally fully equipped, who are well socially connected, are in a hugely advantageous position to dominate the participatory process. It is inevitable for the powerful and resourceful interest groups to make tremendous efforts to manipulate the process and the outcome. It is also possible that consent only means silence, indifference, resignation, ignorance, and all other passive or hopeless mentalities. In a society of inequality, the powerful can produce consent and popular support one way or another. In the end, the only thing a referendum can accomplish is to produce an image of a government by popular consent. Here, the issue is: a democratic popular consent is no different from authoritarian popular consent. Many authoritarian governments have won popular consent one way or another, but they are not democracies after all. All of these issues would expose the shortcomings of direct democracy. It is not only hard to put into practice, but also produces outcomes that are contradictory to its original purpose and ideals.

For democracy to succeed, power must be in the possession of the people. As Rousseau maintains, sovereignty belongs to the people and cannot be transferred by them, even freely, to any other body or people. The key issue is whether the people on different levels of the societal hierarchy can play active roles in the political process. For this purpose, the system must have a high degree of permeability and the people must have the access to the channels of political process. A democratic government is one that can truly go to the people and connect the people in a meaningful way, besides the routine and largely superficial campaign and election. In a society of huge inequality in all aspects of social life, only meaningful and effective social connection can play a role to minimize the negative impact of inequality on the political process and produce popular sovereignty. In this respect, in addition to the Western experience of democracy, the experiences beyond the Western democracy are potentially useful.

Some fundamental questions are still unanswered, such as: who are "the people" who are entrusted with the ultimate authority by the democratic ideal? What is "the genuine will of the people" that is supposed to be the expression of the popular sovereignty? How do "the people" exercise its power over those who distort their will and abuse their rights? And most fundamentally, what is the relationship between "the people" and those "above" them? It is clear the common conceptions are not adequate for us to understand "the true" democracy. As anyone who knows the sound scientific reasoning, we must be able to isolate the key factors and exclude the "third" or "lurking" factors in order to establish a genuine causal relationship. The common mistake we make is that we simply assume whatever we are practicing are the factors that have caused the democratic governance. However, they are very likely the confounding factors, or even coincidence. The argument this chapter is trying to make is that the genuine factors that have caused the democratic governance are the special types of webs of social connections between the socially powerful and the ordinary people. It is "social connection" that serves as the way, the essence and the causal factor of democratic process while all the commonly mentioned factors are the possible confounding factors or false forms.

For example, voting is widely regarded as the cause of democratic practice—if there is a free election, there must be democracy. However, both voting and democracy are confounding factors. The real factor that determines both of them is social connection. If voting can effectively serve as the way for the powerful to connect to the ordinary people, it can facilitate a democratic practice. If voting is superficial and cannot attract sufficient participation, or it simply stimulates disconnection instead of facilitating connection, it will have nothing to do with democratic practice, or even worse.

We cherish the democratic political system; we regard it as the most durable form of governance throughout human history. In the mean time, we also regard its commonly acclaimed forms as false. If the essence and the causal factor of democratic practice is social connection, all the forms that do not serve this factor will eventually lose power and fade into history and the emerging forms that better serve this essence will grow and replace the old ones. If we are not able to predict what the emerging new forms are, we can at least point out the essence that causes the new forms to emerge.

As E. H. Carr insightfully pointed out:

To speak today of the defense of democracy as if we were defending something which we knew and had possessed for many decades or many centuries is self-deceptive and sham. . . The criterion must be sought not in the survival of traditional institutions, but in the question where power resides and how it is exercised. In this respect, democracy is a matter of degree. Some countries today are more democratic than others. But none is perhaps very democratic, if any high standard of democracy is applied. Mass democracy is a difficult and hitherto largely uncharted territory; and we should be nearer the mark, and should have a far more convincing slogan, if we spoke of the need, not to defend democracy, but to create it[14]

DIRECT DEMOCRACY—
THE CASE OF THE ATHENIAN SYSTEM

In the play *The Suppliant Women*, Euripides set out the thesis about direct democracy as it was practiced in Athens. When a foreigner, Herald, asked to see the king and deliver a message from his king Creon, the answer he got was:

> This state is not
> Subject to one man's will, but is a free city.
> The king here is the people, who by yearly office
> Govern in turn. We give no special power to wealth;
> The poor man's voice commands equal authority.

The foreigner had a hard time making sense of it. He replied:

> The city that come from lives under command
> Of one man, not a rabble. . .
> The common man!
> Incapable of plain reasoning, how can he guide
> A city in sound policies? Experience gives
> More useful knowledge than impatience. Your poor rustic,
> Even though he be no fool—how can he turn his mind
> From ploughs to politics?[15]

It is understandable that it is not easy to make sense of a government by amateurs—government positions were filled by lots, all the citizens assembled to make major decisions ten times a year, and people who occupied positions could not continuously occupy them for more than two years in their lives. If we are used to the individualistic perspective and see the state from the utilitarian lens, we would see the negative side of this system just as Plato asserted:

> Now when we meet in the Assembly, then if the State is faced with some building project, I observe that the architects are sent for and consulted about the proposed structures, and when it is a matter of shipbuilding, the naval designers, and so on with everything which the Assembly regards as a subject for learning and teaching . . . But when it is something to do with the government of the country that is to be debated, the man who gets up to advise them may be a

builder or equally well a blacksmith or a shoemaker, merchant or ship-owner, rich or poor, of good family or none. . . . that here is a man who, without any technical qualifications . . . is yet trying to give advice.[16]

He is right if we see the state as a machine that certainly needs experts and specialists to handle it. However, the state is not a machine; it is a human society. The key issue for a human society is how to bring individuals together and keep them together, and more critically, to work together when difficult circumstances arise. This is the essence of any effective political system, no matter what form it takes. Forms of government only serve this essence. Individual ignorance and incompetence is secondary as compared to open debate, equal opportunity of participation and collective wisdom when we think about communal existence. In the case of the Athenian democracy, it played a pivotal role in neutralizing kinship and local allegiances in the critical times of the very survival of the state and kept the citizens loyal to the polis as a whole. Politics is, therefore, a business of mobilizing collective effort, instead of elite domination with the masses left in the dark, let alone the arbitrary and unpredictable rule of despots.

Central to Athenian democracy was active citizenship. It was the organic connections between each individual citizen and the state that made the system work. "Organic connection" means that each citizen was a part of the body polis, who was dependent on the body polis and was not self-sufficient. As Thucydides pointed out: "Here each individual is interested not only in his own affairs but in the affairs of the state as well. . . we do not say that a man who takes no interest in politics is a man who minds his own business: we say that he has no business here at all."[17] As Peter Green mentioned: "To Pericles and his fifth-century contemporaries, the private individual, or idiots, was an idiot in our modern sense, irresponsible because unconcerned with public affairs."[18] Here, communal identity was built up through active participatory democracy in which individuals felt their share of the community and their function in the community.

It is no doubt that the ancient Athenian democracy represents what democracy originally meant and strived to be: the oneness of society and state. "Athenian democracy signified, precisely, the refusal of any division between 'state' and 'society'."[19]

However, this was only in theory. In practice, the problem of the Athenian democracy is not that it did not have specialized experts to run its government and it therefore practiced the "mob rule." Its critical problem was highlighted by its failure to achieve the oneness of state and society—its state did not truly mirror society in its democratic process. In reality, society is never composed of equally existent individuals. We are always divided and our community is always hierarchical. As Anthony Arblaster asserts:

We are not now accustomed to associate democracy with such overt expressions of class hostility and social conflict. The notion that support for democracy might mean taking sides in a kind of class war will seem absurd to most people today. Yet democracy, both in ancient Greece and in the politics of the past two centuries, has never been achieved without a struggle, and that struggle has always been, in good part, a type of class struggle, even if it is very simply characterized, as it was by many Greeks, as a struggle of the many poor against the few who are rich and well-born[20]

Ancient Athenian society, despite the huge effort to minimize the political impact of economic capital still could not limit a reality: from the very beginning, the equal political system existed side by side uneasily with the unequal economic relationship. It is obvious that while money can buy land, houses, and luxury goods for its owner, it can also buy political influence if its owner so wishes. More significantly, money can indirectly buy all the necessary means to make the money holder influential and powerful. Education, skills, manners, leisure time and social connections are all the necessary conditions for a successful public life and all of them require money to obtain. It is true today; it was true in the ancient times in Athens. Indeed, the government (the Council) had no chance to develop into an independent body of dominance and it did not have the institutional possibility to serve a specific class within the people. However, it was only a form. The society it reflected was a mathematic sample of Athens, not the real picture of the dynamic Athens society. As Anthony Arblaster insightfully pointed out:

"Democracy," like so many central terms of politics (including "politics") is in origin a Greek word, combining two shorter words, *demos* and *kratos*. Both terms had more than one meaning. The *demos* could mean the whole citizen body living within a particular polis, or city-state, but might also be used to mean "the mob" or "the rabble" or the "lower orders." *Kratos* could mean either "power" or "rule": the two are not the same. It is perfectly possible to conceive of groups or individuals who have power without actually ruling in the official, visible sense. So a formal democracy, in which the people or the people's representatives appeared to rule, might conceal a very undemocratic distribution of actual power. Or conversely, a political system in which a monarch or an aristocracy formally ruled might disguise the fact that real power was in the hands of the people. This ambiguity in both constituent terms, present at the very birth of the concept and the reality of democracy, is of permanent significance in grasping its meaning and its history.[21]

Thucydides seemed to echo this theme when he described the relationship between Pericles, who was a member of the well-educated upper class, and the populace: "It was he who led them, rather than they who led him . . . So, in what was nominally a democracy, power was really in the hands of the first citizen."[22] Therefore, the essence is not form, but content. The form can be the Athenian direct democracy and the content is power dynamics among all social groups that made Athens as a human community possible. It was the power dynamics among all social groups that connected all the people who could have some impact on the Athenian society by their actions. In this way, the connective power dynamics held all social groups together and made the society possible. The institutionalized political system might facilitate the connections among different social forces in the society at certain times, but it was not flexible enough to reflect the dynamic process of power contests all the time. At any moment that the power dynamics among different social groups (the content) could not exercise themselves smoothly through the institutionalized political system (the form), we see the tension. The very existence of the society was at stake.

As we well know, all the contemporary great philosophers in that era looked at democracy with suspicion. The list includes Plato, Socrates, Aristotle, and Thucydides and many countless others. The case they made against Athenian democracy has clearly highlighted the difficulty of the oneness of state and society. The major issue was that it was virtually impossible for the upper class to organically connect to the lower class, unless the latter accepts the former's control and serves the ends of the former as tools. However, after all, they lived in the same society. They, therefore, had to find a way to live together, stay together and work together, especially when there were foreign threats. The Athenian direct democracy is therefore a valuable experiment that has taught us so much. We see the "bottom up" approach of the connective power dynamics that had forced its way into the Athenian direct democracy; we also see the fierce resistance of the upper class in the process. The upper class eventually institutionalized a "top down" system to connect to the lower class, which channeled the energy of lower class into the political process through connective power dynamics and accomplished the precarious yet dynamic balance in the community. However, the struggle had continuously gone on before it finally weakened the system to an extent that a foreign invasion completely destroyed the whole system. The lesson I learned is twofold: first, I must be a realist in order to see the power dynamics that work to shape social reality; second, I must be an idealist in order to look beyond the immediate reality and see the "bottom up" power through connection that has the potential to affect the power dynamics in the future. In any case, we see that social connection is the essence of the Athenian type of democracy.

REPRESENTATIVE DEMOCRACY—
THE CASE OF THE AMERICAN SYSTEM

It might be safe to say that the American democratic system reflects more accurately the political reality than the Athenian system. At the period between the *Declaration of Independence* in 1776 and the Philadelphia Constitutional Convention in 1787, there was considerable pressure to establish the Athenian type of direct democracy with popular participation. Thomas Paine was one of the democrats who spoke for the menial types for constant elections and popular referendums.[23] However, the Founding Fathers were more concerned with real politics. They, like the British conservative Edmund Burk, keenly discerned the real political power as grounded in the propertied. They therefore established a system to restrain the popular will, to restrict the franchise to property-holders and to protect the participation of the rich and propertied while sacrificing the menial types such as butchers, carpenters, etc. Even the most radical among them, including Thomas Jefferson, defined "the people" as propertied when they proclaimed their faith in "the people." Jefferson's famous argument that "173 despots would surely be as oppressive as one"[24] echoed Burke's "The tyranny of the multitude is but a multiplied tyranny."[25] What they wanted was clearly not "a democracy" but "a republic." Hamilton made this point even more clear. He asserted at the Philadelphia Convention that "Give all power to the many, they will oppress the few. Give all the power to the few, they will oppress the many." He thus supported the idea to give "the rich and well-born" a "distinct, permanent share in the government" through which they could "check the imprudence of democracy."[26]

The ideal of American representative democracy is therefore not a government of the people and by the people. It is a government of "the best and the brightest" chosen by the people to govern them. As long as the institutionalized political system is flexible enough to connect the powerful and the ordinary people, it would better reflect the structure of real political power in the society and therefore achieve a higher degree of oneness between state and society. Because of this, it has the institutional set-up to potentially do better for the people than the Athenian direct democracy.

However, since the representative democratic system focuses on controlling the abuse of power by public officials, not wealthy citizens as was designed by Hamilton, Madison and others, the system does not address the issue of inequality on the societal level. The fundamental issue therefore remains: the rule of congruence works powerfully in the political process: money can buy power and power can transfer into money.[27] Effective social connection between the powerful and the ordinary is therefore weak. Without genuine connection in the society, the oneness of state and society is still far away from reality. In fact, the lack of social connection in the democratic process because of the impact of economic inequality is an increasing problem in the contemporary American political system.[28] It is clear that the poor and the menial types do have some power in society, but their power is rooted in their social functions as part of the society. As romantic poet Byron stated:

You call these men a mob, desperate, dangerous, and ignorant . . . Are we aware of our obligation to a mob? It is the mob that labour in your fields and serve in your houses,—that man your navy and recruit your army,—. . . You many call the people a mob; but do not forget that a mob too often speaks the sentiments of the people.[29]

He, in fact, highlighted a political truth: the ordinary people are not powerless. They are part of the society and each of them separately plays important function in the society. However, they cannot play their functions without positioning themselves in a hierarchically constructed social system. They consequently connect to the powerful in countless ways. But the democratic political system needs to focus on promoting genuine social connections. If the political system, the state, does not alienate them too disproportionately and therefore facilitates their connections to the powerful, the democracy will grow. Otherwise, the power structure of the society will be skewed completely and the very foundation of representative democracy will be shattered.

It is commonly regarded that in the system of representative democracy, election can be an effective means for the ordinary people to make an impact on the political process. After all, they are in the majority and if each individual in the majority votes for his/her own interests, s/he will make the system work for her/him. Therefore, universal suffrage seems the ultimate solution to the potential problem of representation. James Mill was the person who made this point most clearly in his classic *Essay on Government*. As he asserted, since the few "aristocracies" cannot be trusted for the general good, and the mass assemblies are not practical, the best form of government is representative. Elections must be frequent in order to check the representatives. Mill believed that it was through the representative frequent election system that the powerful and the ordinary could be brought into accord.[30]

However, history suggests that, instead of producing working-class political domination, as so many nineteenth century liberals, including the younger Mill, worried, universal suffrage has had little impact on the dominance of the rich and powerful.[31] Hence, it has had little effect on minimizing the alienation of the ordinary people in the political process. What is worrisome is that representative democracy, with election as its major instrument of connection between the powerful and the ordinary people, cannot effectively connect all the social forces that are more or less powerful in the societal process. The rule of congruence is salient and a large segment of social forces is marginalized and alienated under the system of representative democracy.

It might not be easy to discern this worrisome situation in ordinary times. But two World Wars highlighted the power of the ordinary people and the necessity to effectively connect them to the dominant class. In each human community across the Western World where representative democracy has been practiced for more than one hundred years, the politically powerful realized the weakness in this regard. As President Woodrow Wilson mentioned: "Sacrifices could be demanded in the name of democracy which could not be expected for mere patriotism for the social order as it was."[32]

But, once the dust settled down, the sentiment that dislikes or fears mass participation keeps causing loud and continuous clamor. Influential theorists, like William Kornhauser, Walter Lippmann, Joseph Schumpeter, S. M. Lipset, Robert Dahl and Samuel Huntington all followed J. S. Mill's footsteps and argued against engaging the general public in the political process.[33] For them, the ordinary people's only task is to elect their representatives; then it is the representatives' duty to govern in whatever ways they see fit. The ordinary people deserve to be passive and should be kept that way. It is clear that within the framework of representative democracy, the efforts to bring the rich and powerful and the ordinary people into accord has reached its limit. The connection between the two social forces can only reach a certain degree and social mobilization, social integration, and societal coherence have thus failed to reach the maximum. It would be impossible for the state and society to reach oneness under representative democracy. A new paradigm is therefore called for to provide a theoretical framework to the effort to more effectively connect all social forces across society.

CONNECTIVE DEMOCRACY AND GLOBAL GOVERNANCE

We discussed two major types of democracy in the literature of contemporary political science: representative, or institutional, democracy and participatory, or direct, democracy. The former is materialized by the contemporary "democratic states" with the US as the model and the latter is exercised in ancient Athens and only in the form of small town meetings or small group activities in the contemporary world. It is clear that both of them are limited by either national borders or small social circles. Representative democracy has been facilitating a social reach on the national scale for elite groups to control the general population inside nation-states in current democratic states, whereas participatory democracy helps local elites to set agendas and implement local control. They have also developed some principles of democracy. But, the problem is that it is impossible for either of them to achieve social reach globally.

The weakness of the American system in terms of setting up an example for an effective form of global governance is likely to be its institutionalized effort to promote representative, or institutional, democracy globally. This is not likely to be a fertile effort. The reason is very clear: the institution of representative democracy is, by its nature, strictly limited to the space within national borders. It is impossible to achieve cross border social reach based on representative democracy. Even inside the national borders, the American polity functions much less well in enriching social capital and facilitating civic engagement. As Putnam insightfully pointed out: Without sufficient social connection, the most likely results are: a Perot-style electronic town hall, a kind of plebiscitary democracy, isolated individual voices without engaging with one another; citizenship as a spectator sport; politics at a distance; alienation, apathy, and the less availability of informal networks among citizens of different social strata. It is the citizenship by proxy and government by the professionals. The key issue is: empowerment between the representatives and the people they represent are lacking.[34]

The only thing that can travel across national borders is the democratic ideology, the soft power. But it has diffuse effects on other nations and unforeseeable consequences for America. The policy of promoting representative democracy constantly ends in a difficult dilemma: it is impossible to balance ideology and practical necessity. The current situation in Palestine is a very good example: a strictly democratically elected government with a terrorist group as its leader.

This weakness contributed to a very strange situation in the US led governance system: America is strong in terms of both "hard" power and "soft" power—we are the only superpower militarily and economically, and the American way of life, including the democratic ideal, is the dominant ideology, but both of these hard and soft powers cannot carry a governance system far. We are not able to solve the Iran nuclear, as well as other, issue effectively; we labor very hard but only watch the situation worsening in Palestine; we cannot even keep our own backyard unified and peaceful (as is clear when we look at the current situation in Latin America). The situation in Africa does not look favorable and the big countries, like France, Germany, China, Russia, and even Japan, are increasingly claiming their own power independently from the US. The only success story is the resolution on North Korea's unclear issue. This story highlights that to tackle the issues of global governance, social reach is essential.

Connective democracy with all the social constructions embedded in the institutions of global capitalism as its carrier would be the most effective way to promote global democracy and peace because connective democracy as a political institution is embedded in all types of global social reach without the limitation of national borders. Politically, for better or for worse (depending on where you stand), the future of the 21st century belongs to connective democracy. As one drop of water in the river of endless history, the 21st century with connective democracy as its signature accomplishment will be the milestone for promoting ever-expanding social reach throughout human history.

Connective democracy starts with its answer to a key question: Does "the general will" exist at all in reality? Connective democracy goes beyond the dichotomy of individuals vs. community and focuses on social capital accumulation through social connections in community life. It regards social connections as the precondition for the realization of all democratic principles. As John Dewey mentioned: "Fraternity, liberty and equality isolated from communal life are hopeless abstractions. . . . Democracy must begin at home, and its home is the neighborly community."[35] William Kornhauser also pointed out: "People divorced from community, occupation, and association are first and foremost among the supporters of extremism."[36] Robert Putnam highlighted the connection between the possession of social capital and the practice of democracy: social connections function in a democratic system in the following ways: instilling habits of cooperation and public-spiritedness; playing the role of democratic education as the "schools for democracy;" facilitating all the civic virtues—trustworthiness, reciprocity, active participation, fair-mindedness, concerns for generalized other. All of these important elements of democracy are developed through social connections and social capital strengthens our better, more expansive selves.[37]

In domestic politics, there are two approaches to construct the social connections. First is the top-down approach—teaching through establishing social connections and accumulating social capital by the established upper social groups that facilitates an engaging and learning process. The connections, once established, will have the power to force everybody involved to think deeper and concern wider. The second is the bottom-up approach, i.e., deliberative democracy: the lower social groups of people push for a more inclusive system by widening the circle of participation. Both approaches are effective depending on a key issue: a polity must be the faithful reflection of the society. For connective democracy, both individual based "the will of all" and the "the general will of the community" are pure theoretical illusions. They do not exist in reality. It is obvious that in reality, for the purpose of reflecting "the will of all," if the minority is granted veto power on the grounds of the principles of freedom and pluralism, the system will surely be paralyzed. Equally obviously, "the will of the majority" is not same as "the general will."

The only will is "the connective will." It is the result of the ever-changing connective power dynamic based on both top-down and bottom-up processes. There is no intrinsic interest or will of either individuals or the community. The political interests and will are changeable, flexible, and fluid. The whole process of "will or interest formation" depends on the patterns of social connection and the power dynamics derived from them. In political reality, both individual drive toward his/her self-constructed interests or will and the altruistic selfless sense of community are only "raw" materials. It is the interaction between individuals and groups that matters. Everyone, including the majority, is only part of the web of connections. Individual self interest and will are formulated, shaped, and framed though a process of interactions in a patterned connective web. Individuals also eventually realize what is in common among them. As a result, "the general will" of the community emerges. The whole process is dominated by the power of connection—an unbalanced, asymmetrical, mutual, active and applied force which is able to reach out and penetrate in the lives of everybody involved. In the end, it is neither individual will nor general will which prevails; it is the connective will that dictates the political process.

Connective democracy is relationship-based. It focuses on the process of stable, continuous, and free connections between the people on different levels of the societal ladder. It enshrines social relations, rather than individual interests, and regards solid social connections as the most fundamental political unit of action. The concept of "connective democracy" can therefore be defined as the following: connective democracy is a political institution that is embedded in social elites' social connections among different social groups. It is materialized through the social ties between socially elite groups and ordinary citizens. Political power in this system is manifested by social power, i.e. political power is based on social capital and only the people who possess sufficient social capital can be the members of the elite social group and gain political power in society.

Connective Democracy is embedded in a relational web with connective power dynamics that enables the strong while empowering the weak: inclusive but less free; connecting but less equal. The principles of establishing effective social relationships that make social connections possible facilitate an effective political global system. The essence of democracy is connection between the powerful and the powerless. It differs from representative democracy in that the political power in the latter is derived from legal construction, material resource competition, and elite cultural manipulation, whereas the power of the former is socially based. It differs from participatory democracy in that it does not enshrine equality as its most fundamental principle. A hierarchical system is a necessary condition for its operation. However, the hierarchy is not based on material resources or any individualistic characteristics. It is based on the social connections of people. The meaning of "democracy" is about the service of the public and the means to enforce this end is through social rewards or punishments. Everybody is supposed to get involved in the process of forming social ties, but not everybody participates in the political process equally. There are two social factors that determine people's degree of political participation. First is an interpersonal factor: people who gain more community trust and thus accumulate more social power (capital) would participate more. People with bad social reputations and selfish, ego-centric people would not gain much political power. Second is the structural factor: people with the right strength of social ties or people at the advantageous "structure hole" positions would get more access to political power.

Power here is not manifested by position and ability to judge, to award, or to punish, but by position and the ability to become socially involved in people's daily lives through social connections. It is highlighted by the position and ability to share responsibilities and solve problems together with a wide variety of social groups. Also, as the concept of connective authority would highlight, power is not legitimated by legal, traditional, or charismatic means for power-holders to stay aloof in the high places and look down to judge, to award, and to punish. It gains its legitimacy by social connection and involvement.

The significance of this type of political institution for domestic politics is its power to reduce the fragmentation created by both representative and participatory democracy. It therefore has the power to form a national connective power dynamic to unify the nation on a deeper level and enhance the political control of elite groups in a social and more fundamental way. Globally, connective democracy facilitates social reach on the global scale. Connective democracy is a form that has the greatest potential to enable a new form of global governance. As we mentioned above, there is no barrier that can fundamentally block the expansion of social connections. Clearly, we can see the competition among elite groups against each other for global social reach. There will be many conflicts, but the conflicts are social in nature. The unit of elite control will no longer be the nation-state, but the social sphere. To control a larger social sphere across national borders and in order to be winners in the conflicts, an elite group has to be socially functional and follow structurally institutionalized social ways.

Therefore the "triple test" devised in Morgenthau's theory for specific forms of government is no longer applicable. It is not about whether "the peoples of the world are willing to accept it" or not; it is not about whether they are "willing and able to do what is necessary to keep world government standing"; it is not about whether they are "willing and able to do or refrain from doing what the global governance system requires of them so that it may fulfill its purposes."[38] The global governance system is democratic because it is the best form of governance that most effectively involves and connects most social groups in the political process. In the mean time, it is the functional and relational connections that make individuals act through the web of international ties. The global governance system in a form of connective democracy therefore represents a higher level mechanism beyond individual members of the global village. Its operation is not based on individual members' willingness or ability. The mechanism works independently from each individual member and frames her or his way of action through her or his position in the connective web.

Here, we might have to answer the questions raised by Putnam: Can Liberty, Equality, Fraternity, these three good things of democracy go together? Is too much fraternity bad for liberty and equality? Is social connections at war with liberty and tolerance? Is social capital at war with equality? Is fraternity in some sense at war with itself?[39] Putnam answered his own questions. Based on the discussions above, I believe his answers about the relationship between social connection–fraternity—and liberty or equality are applicable not only to domestic politics, but also to international relations as well:

> Individuals who are more engaged with their communities are generally more tolerant than their stay-at-home neighbors, not less.[40]
>
> Social joiners and civic activists are as a rule more tolerant of dissent and unconventional behavior than social isolates are.[41]
>
> Community and equality are mutually reinforcing, not mutually incompatible.[42]
>
> Social capital may help produce equality. Historically social capital has been the main weapon of the have-nots, who lacked other forms of capital. 'Solidarity forever' is a proud, strategically sensible rally cry for those, such as ethnic minorities or the working class, who lack access to conventional political clout. So it is plausible that well-knit communities can sustain more egalitarian social and political arrangements.[43]

If we substitute nation-states for individuals in the statements above, we can see social connections among nation-states can produce the same result as it has proven to be able to produce among individuals. The key issue might be whether fraternity is more likely to be at war with each other. It is true that, as Putnam pointed out, "Fraternity is most natural within socially homogeneous groups." "Social divisiveness is the central normative issue raised by communitarianism." "Some kinds of bonding social capital may discourage the formation of bridging social capital and vice versa."[44] For Putnam, "for our biggest collective problems we need precisely the sort of bridging social capital that is toughest to create."[45]

However, this issue is not irresolvable. On the surface, "fraternity" has two elements of connection in it. The first is "bonding"—the human community composed of homogeneous members and the second is "bridging"—the connection between those "homogeneous communities." The key term here is "homogeneity." But in reality homogeneity is only a matter of degree. No social group is purely homogeneous—even a family is divided by gender, age, and status. For a purpose of resource maintenance, people have to stay together no matter how different they are. We see many more conflicts within a family than in any other social groups but family members are still together, rather closely. Nation-state is a modern form of tribalism. Its homogeneity depends on its institutional construction of the uniqueness and distinctiveness. The competitive advantage of the "structure holes" as they developed in the process of globalization has already eroded the institutionalization of the uniqueness and distinctiveness of each nation-state. The construction of a connective democracy will erode it more as each nation-state strives to fulfill its purpose of resource maintenance and expansion. Since "bridging" is more effective for resource expansion through the exponential nature of social capital accumulation, connective democracy will gain its global power as a governance system-in-being.

NOTES

1. Hans J. Morgenthau, *Politics among Nations: the strength for power and peace,* seventh edition (Boston MA: McGraw Hill, 2006): 516.

2. Hans J. Morgenthau, 514.

3. Hans J. Morgenthau, 511.

4. Hans J. Morgenthau, 506.

5. Hans J. Morgenthau, 510.

6. Hans J. Morgenthau, 509.

7. Hans J. Morgenthau, 509.

8. Hans J. Morgenthau, 334.

9. Hans J. Morgenthau, 515.

10. C. B. Macpherson, *The Real World of Democracy* (Oxford: Clarendon Press, 1966): 1.

11. Jean-Jacques Rousseau, Du Contrat Social, Book IV, Ch. 2. In Anthony Arblaster, *Democracy* (Minneapolis: University of Minnesota Press, 1987): 69.

12. D. H. Lawrence, "Democracy," in *Selected Essays,* (Harmondsworth: Penguin Books, 1950): 78.

13. Nan Lin, *Social Capital: a theory of social structure and action,* (Cambridge, UK: Cambridge University Press, 2001), Chapter 5.

14. E. H. Carr, in Anthony Arblaster, 105.

15. Euripides, *The Suppliant Women,* in Orestes and other plays, trans. Philip Vellancott, (Harmondsworth: Penguin Book, 1972): 206-07.

16. Plato, Protagoras, in *Protagoras and Meno,* trans. W.K.C. Guthrie, (Harmondsworth: Penguin Books, 1956): 50–51 and 53–54.

17. Thucydides, *The Peloponnesian War,* trans. John Warrington (London: Dent Everyman, 1959): 118-119.

18. Peter Green, *A concise History of Ancient Greece* (London: Thames & Hudson, 1973): 79.

19. Perry Anderson, *Passages From Antiquity to Feudalism* (London: New Left Books, 1974): 43.

20. Anthony Arblaster, 14.

21. Anthony Arblaster, 13.

22. Thucydides, 134.

23. Thomas Paine, *Common Sense* (Harmondsworth: Penguin Books, 1976).

24. Thomas Jefferson, "Notes on the State of Virginia," in *The Portable Thomas Jefferson,* ed. Merrill D. Peterson (Harmondsworth: Penguin Books, 1977): 164.

25. Edmund Burke, *Reflections on the Revolution in France* (Harmondsworth: Penguin Book, 1968): 141.

26. Robert B. Morris, ed. *Alexander Hamilton and the Founding of the Nation* (New York: Harper Torchback, 1969): 154 and 152; Max Farrand, ed. *The Records of the Federal Convention of 1787,* vols. I–III (New Haven, CT.: Yale University Press, 1966); Alexander Hamilton, James Madison, and John Jay, *The Federalist*, with the Letters of "Brutus." Ed. Terence Ball, (Cambridge UK.: Cambridge University Press, 2003) nos. 10 and 51.

27. Nan Lin, 38-39.

28. Steve Fraser and Gary Gerstle, ed. *Ruling America: A History of Wealth and Power in a Democracy* (Cambridge, MA: Harvard University Press, 2005); Paul Krugman, *The Great Unravelling: Losing Our Way in a New Century* (New York, NY.: W.W. Norton & Company, 2003).

29. Byron, *Selected Prose*, ed. Peter Gunn (Harmondsworth: Penguin Books, 1972): 111.

30. James Mill, *Utilitarian Logic and Politics*, ed. Jack Lively and John Rees, (Oxford: Clarendon Press, 1978): 59.

31. Adam Przeworski, Susan C. Stokes, and Bernard Manin, ed. *Democracy, Accountability, and Representation* (Cambridge, UK: Cambridge University Press, 1999).

32. In Bernard Crick, *In Defense of Politics* (London: Weidnenfeld & Nicolson, 1962): 67.

33. The conservative theorists including the influential theorists, like William Kornhauser (*The Politics of Mass Society,* London: Routledge & Kegan Paul, 1960), Walter Lippmann (*The Public Philosophy,* New York: Mentor Books, 1956), Joseph Schumpeter (*Capitalism, Socialism and Democracy,* London: George Allen & Unwin, 1943), S. M. Lipset (*Political Man,* London: Heinemann, 1960), Robert Dahl (*Dilemmas of Pluralist Democracy,* London: Yale University Press, 1982) and Samuel Huntington ("The Democratic Distemper," *The Public Interest* 39, Spring 1975). All of them followed J. S. Mill's (J.S. Mill, *On Liberty*, ed. Gertrude Himmelfarb, Harmondsworth: Penguin Books, 1974) in arguing that mass participation is harmful to representative democracy.

34. Robert Putnam, *Bowling Alone* (New York: Simon & Shuster, 2000): 341.

35. John Dewey, in Robert Putnam, 337.

36. William Kornhauser, in Robert Putnam, 338.

37. Robert Putnam, 338–39.

38. Hans J. Morgenthau, 514.

39. Robert Putnam, Chapter 22.
40. Robert Putnam, 355.
41. Robert Putnam, 355.
42. Robert Putnam, 358.
43. Robert Putnam, 358.
44. Robert Putnam, 362.
45. Robert Putnam, 362.

Conclusion

A Connectivist Construction
of American Identity
and Global Leadership

WHO ARE WE?

It is impossible to conduct international relations without first clarifying the identity issue. Who are we? Or, who is the United States of America? What role is it supposed to play in world affairs? The realists would say: the United States is the strongest and most powerful nation-state in the world. If we accept this identity, the steps we will follow to conduct ourselves in international relations will naturally be focused on the unilaterally determined "national interests" in order to keep the United States the strongest and most powerful nation-state. All we need to do is to come up with clearly defined national interests based on enhancing the military and economic power and realize them by utilizing whatever power is at our disposal.

However, the idealists would say that America is a nation with a clear destination. Therefore, their construction of the identity of the United States of America is that it is the beacon of hope to peoples around the world. Our values, including the American style democratic political system, our market economy and our ideal of freedom, are universally applicable. They are so attractive to people around the world that they long for a liberal democratic political system, a part of our economic system, and freedom. All of this can only be bestowed by the United States of America. Also, hard power is far from enough; our identity as a nation with a destination reflects our soft power. The foreign policy based upon this identity would naturally focus on promoting democratic nation-states, developing economic relationships through market mechanisms, and propagandizing the ideology of individual freedom and human rights. The United States would be a world police force, safeguarding justice against human rights violations across the globe.

Constructivists would insist that how people think about the reality actually shapes it. The issue of identity is about shared ideas and intersubjective discourse. Therefore, it is fluid. It depends on how the major players construct the discourse based on their subjective understandings and interpretations of reality. The power of both "hard" power and "soft" power is based on how the players frame them and make sense of them. The policy consequences of this line of thinking would naturally be focused on intersubjective mind shaping in the international public sphere.

I would like to offer a connectivist alternative to these prevailing ways of thinking. In my view, the identity of the United States of America is a functional and relational global leader. T. D. Jakes's comments in the 150th anniversary issue of *Atlantic Monthly* on "the American idea" is not only inspiring, but also best illustrates the point of departure of my connectivist view and highlights the difference between my connectivist view and realism. According to him, "One hundred fifty years ago, it was easier for this country to put its owns needs first, middle, and last. But no longer can the world's most prosperous nation pursue happiness irrespective to a global economy, a planet's stewardship, and the health of peoples in country after country after country. Our challenge now is to strength ourselves as a nation that is inextricably tied to a world of nations."[1] Anne-Marie Slaughter's comments in the same issue highlights the point of departure of my connectivist view and its difference from the idealism. As she puts it: "Today we are but one facet of a many-faceted global experiment—a status we should embrace as the hallmark of our initial success."[2]

A functional and relational leader is different from being the strongest member; different from being a value originator and enforcer; different from being an economic power-house or major ideological attraction; and also different from being an intellectual center that dominates the public discourse. Of course, without both hard and soft powers and without the advantageous position in intersubjective discourse, it is impossible to be a leader. But all the factors mentioned by the three dominant theories are necessary conditions. They are not sufficient to make a nation-state the global leader, no matter how powerful it is. The real sufficient condition or factor that makes a nation-state the global leader is the power of connection. Only the nation-state(s) in the functional position in the international structure that are consciously developing relational connections to other nation-states can possess this power. It includes two kind of connections: functional connection and relational connection. The power of connection manifests itself in two ways: first is as the central position in the overall global economic, political and military structure—the marginalized strongest member cannot be the leader; second is the effective inter-governmental connections it builds that enable it to play a functional role—the isolated strongest member cannot be the leader.

The key issue for the United States to address to assume the identity of a global leader is not based on any unique characteristics America as an individual nation possesses; instead, it is based on its position in the web of international ties and its effectiveness in seeking connections. There are two sides of the process of leadership construction: first, the leader accepts the structure as it is and positions itself at the center of the structure; second, the leader actively constructs a structure that is centered around it. The first is primary and the second is secondary. But anyway, the leader cannot successfully achieve its leadership identity through its individualistic "hard" or "soft" power.

The fact that America is the global leader at this point in history is not because of its financial or military power, not because of its moral values or its power to shape international discourse. It is because of its functional position in the international structure and the connections it has made. Using Talcott Parson's structural-functional theory,[3] we can say that the US has been playing key roles in the four survival requisites of human society:

As the engine of global economy, it has been facilitating human adaptation to the natural environment in order to gain sufficient facilitates through its productive economic machine and scientific exploration;

As the center of global intellectual discourse, it has been leading human goal attainment for human society to gain the ability to prioritize goals and to mobilize resources to accomplish them;

As the most active agent and coordinator of global integration, it has been supporting the integration of human society through market economy and international institutions for human society to develop the ability to coordinate and sustain viable relationships among individual units;

And as the only powerful force with the capacity to reach every corner of the globe, it has been playing a key role in latency to exercise social control, pattern maintenance and tension management.

Also, using Robert D. Putnam, Nan Lin and other network theorists' theories,[4] we can say that the US has accumulated a sufficient amount of social capital through its tremendous international efforts since World War I. It has therefore occupied the key position in the web of international ties. This structural position has enabled it to possess the highest reachability while other nation-states are localized in their limited spheres. The US is one of the very few, if not the only, nation-state that has the structural connection to socially reach most key players across the globe.

These two aspects, functional connection and relational connection, have made it possible for America to be a global leader, regardless of whether people recognize it or not. It is clear that not everyone recognizes this true source of effective leadership. There exists a clear incompatibility between the objective role the US is playing in the world and the subjective consciousness about how to play this role. For many policy makers and high level think tank people, striving for being the strongest and the most powerful is still the dominant policy goal; for some others, it is the ideological-moral dominance that is most worthwhile of pursuit. Based on my connectivist vision, I would say American foreign policy must be centered on one single question: how to be better connected functionally and relationally in the global structure for the purpose of being an effective global leader? This is the reason we need to think about the necessity of discussing the issue of social reach in global power dynamics. This is an objective task placed on the shoulders of the US by history, no matter whether we recognize it or not, no matter whether we want to do it or not.

My connectivist approach is grounded in my vision that the world is a small village—it is not an anarchic field where everyone is out for themselves; it is not an interdependent market place where people are connected to each other and the most important thing to do is to set up rules and establish institutions to enforce the rules. Therefore, global leadership is about how to be an effective village head. As we know, a village head can never be a strong man single-mindedly pursuing his own strategic interests; also, he cannot be a self-indulging person with his own moral value as the only destination of everybody else. The strongest fighter or the smartest merchant cannot be an effective village head. Instead, he must be functionally and relationally connected to every household in the village and he must be a functional and relational leader. To further illustrate my vision, I would like to analyze the two champion 2008 presidential candidates' statements about foreign policy. It is commonly understood that the foreign policy formulations by the presidential candidates reflect both the highest level contemporary policy construction and the most possible future policy orientation. In the July/August 2007 issue of *Foreign Affairs*, Barack Obama and Mitt Romney provide us with their detailed foreign policy formulations.[5] I shall start with Barack Obama.

A CONNECTIVIST RESPONSE TO OBAMA

Global Leadership

Obama's title is "Renewing American Leadership." I believe it is a good title, but do not think he is clear about the sociological meaning of "leadership." Without theoretical consistency, he has offered many conflicting statements and solutions.

I agree with Obama's assessment about the tasks we are facing today: This century's threats are as dangerous as those we have confronted in the past:

weapons of mass destruction, global terrorists, rogue states, rising powers, weak states, a warming planet.[6] However, I would say some of his solutions deviated from the connectivist perspective.

I found that Obama's notion that "To see American power in terminal decline is to ignore our great promise and historic purpose"[7] is inspiring. I share with Obama in that "the security and well-being of each and every American depends on the security and well-being of those who live beyond our borders. The mission of the United States is to provide global leadership grounded in the understanding that the world shares a common security and a common humanity."[8] I believe Obama sensed the significance of connectedness. He mentioned that "After thousands of lives lost and billions of dollars spent, many Americans may be tempted to turn inward and cede our leadership in world affairs. But this is a mistake we must not make. America cannot meet the threats of this century alone, and the world cannot meet them without America. We can neither retreat from the world nor try to bully it into submission. We must lead the world by deed and by example."[9] Yes, it is true that we cannot retreat from world affairs; we must provide leadership. But in addition to leading by deed and example, we must lead by finding our appropriate position in the overall structure of world affairs and by putting others in their appropriate positions and involving them effectively.

First of all, leadership does not mean being a visionary strong man, standing tall with the vision and power to direct others, fulfilling his purpose as well as the common good. It is about being a man with sense and sensibility to his structural position and functionally behaving compatibly to that position. A leader is not to be distinguished from others; he is the most structurally functional one among many. In his first paragraph, Obama talks about Franklin Roosevelt, Harry Truman, and John F. Kennedy. It is true that they were effective leaders. But the reason for their success was not as Obama described.

For Roosevelt, it was true that he built the most formidable military that defeated the Nazis and that his Four Freedoms gave purpose to the struggle against fascism. For Truman, it was true that his military buildups and the Marshall Plan played critical role as center pieces of the new architecture of the new global structure to respond to the Soviet threat and secure the peace and well-being of nations around the world. For Kennedy, it was true that his modernization of military doctrine and creation of the Peace Corp and the Alliance for Progress worked in dealing with the Soviet Union's unclear power and the crumbling of colonialism. However, I cannot agree with Obama's conclusion. For Obama, their success is that "they used our strength to show people everywhere America at its best."[10] This is a typical "hard power" pluses "soft power" approach. For me, I would say that these three presidents' successes were because they were sensitive to the structural position American had occupied and acted compatibly with that position. To Obama, "strength" and showing strength is the key. Yes, it is obvious that you cannot do anything without strength. But it is not the key. The key is how you react to the specific structural position with strength—your structural position determines how and how much you develop your strength and how you utilize it. Without mentioning the connection between America's structural position at those critical points in history and the ways of developing and showing its strength in a way of connecting to the system as a whole, Obama overlooked a critical issue of leadership.

The Iraqi Issue

Apparently, the first issue we would have to deal with is the Iraqi situation. There is no doubt that, as Obama said, "In the wake of Iraq and Abu Ghraib, the world has lost trust in our purpose and our principles."[11] According to the connectivist perspective, even if we win the battle (we are capable of sending in enough troops and forcing all the warring factions in Iraq into submission), we still lose the war because we have lost the war at the beginning even before we started the invasion. I therefore share with Obama that the war "should never have been authorized and never should have been waged."[12] However, according to Obama, the wrong reason for the Bush administration to wage the war was that "The Bush administration responded to the unconventional attacks of 9/11 with conventional thinking of the past, largely viewing problems as state-based and principally amendable to military solutions."[13] I disagree with this view because of the following reasons.

First, the word "respond" is not accurate. The Iraq war is an offensive action instead of a defensive one. It is the Bush administration's grand strategy of seizing the opportunity of the aftermath of 9/11 to launch a global offensive to expand American interests as they defined them. Second, the theoretical framework of the Bush administration's offensive action includes the view about the role of state but is much deeper than it. It is, rather, a combination of offensive realism and idealism (in a form of neo-conservativism). For the former, a state must seize every opportunity to make itself stronger and more powerful—balance of power is not enough to secure its security. For the latter, liberal democracy and market force are invincible. The way to secure a peaceful world is to shape it with liberal democratic ideals. This is the root of Bush's theoretical inconsistency because, after all, these two theories cannot work together. The very essence of democracy is to let people decide their own fate and their own way of conducting their affairs. It would be a joke to talk about democracy under occupation.

It is clear that the Bush administration has abandoned the pursuit of democracy in the process of trying to win the military battle. But the key difference between the connectivist view and the offensive realism is about how to be a leader. Even if, a big if, we win all the military battles with our far superior military might, and we have a very strong economy that can sustain us through whatever we do, regardless of how costly it might be, can we then be the effective world leader? The answer is definitely no. I say we lost the Iraqi war not because the war itself is not winnable on the battle field, but because we waged the war for the wrong purpose. I therefore agree with Obama's phased withdrawal proposal. But the key issue is how to prevent even bigger chaos in Iraq and beyond. I do not think Obama is clear about this point. The connectivist approach is clear: Think about what a village head would do after he mistakenly broke into a family, removed its head, and created chaos. If we give up the illusion of a strong man and take the connectivist approach, we would see clearly that the best way and probably the only way to deal with this mess is to disentangle from it, be an outsider and amass all the neighbors together to put the family back in order. The village head here must be a very friendly facilitator who does not have any bias towards anybody—including all the warring factions inside the family and the conflicting neighbors. The village head must very sensitively put himself in the proper position in the power structure and go with the flow of power. The infighting inside the family might last for a while, but the village head has grasped the possibility to lead everybody through the dark tunnel to see the light.

The Middle East

As to the bigger picture in the Middle East as a whole, I strongly disagree with Obama's idea that "Our starting point must always be a clear and strong commitment to the security of Israel, our strongest ally in the region and its only established democracy."[14] As a village leader with immense power at his disposal, if he has a strong bias in favor of one side of the conflict to begin with, how can he facilitate a compromise? If he artificially drew a line that divides enemy and friend based solely on his personal taste, can he effectively involve all the parties in the conflict? If we truly care about Israel's security instead of simply using it as a tool for our wrongly constructed purpose, we must put it in the proper position in the power structure too.

It seems that to deal with Iran is a sticky business. But if we look at the region as a whole and try our best to take care the entire region instead of individual members, we would see that if we do not try to isolate Iran on purpose, we have the power and leverage to lead Iran onto the right track. Obama talked about diplomacy, but his vision was limited. Diplomacy is only a tool to accomplish some purposes. If the purpose is not right, diplomacy would only facilitate a wrong course. We might need the sense of purpose, as well as the courage, that President Nixon displayed when he broke the ice with Communist China in the early 1970s. President Nixon did not necessarily like Communist China—he was an anti-communist all his life, but he abandoned the one (Taiwan) he liked and approached the one he did not like, with a clear purpose. And his purpose was based on his global vision. Here, flexibility is a strength instead of a weakness. If we have the ability to make ourselves do what we are supposed to do instead of indulging ourselves in what we like to do, we can see a sure sign of our power and strength.

The Military

Obama next talked about the military. It is well known that the military is a very powerful weapon; the more powerful it is, the more careful we have to be when we use it. When we create the military, build it up, and utilize its mighty power, we must have a clear purpose. Obama laid out two purposes of our military: to protect American people or our vital interests and to provide for the common security that underpins global stability. Here we see the ambiguity of his position. When President Bush launched the war on Iraq, it was clear to many people, if not most people, that the war was to protect American people and our vital interests. If the military did a perfect job of forcing the Iraqis to submission, President Bush would have been able to easily justify the war and claim "mission accomplished." But in fact, even if we had not gotten into as much trouble as we have in Iraq, the war was still a losing cause before it even began. According the connectivist perspective, the reason is that we cannot separate the security of American people and the American vital interests from common security and global stability. The former is embedded in the latter. It seems to me that Obama sensed this point but did not further clarify it. If we do not compromise our view to domestic politics, we should say that the purpose of our military is to provide the common security across the globe—that is the most effective way of protecting American people and America's vital interests.

Obama mentioned many items here that need to be invested in and developed. They can be summarized in two areas: the quantity of the military and its equipment. But he failed to distinguish the most important item for our military development: the human capital. The US military is a respectable organization. Its major strength is its capability to transform individuals and make them more valuable in terms of human capital through their military experience. To accomplish the purpose of securing global stability, the military must be able to defeat enemies in a short period of time with a high level of efficiency and mobility. To be able to train high quality people is the key factor. All the equipment must serve the purpose of making the people who handle them more effective. Enlarging the quantity must not sacrifice the quality. If we enlarge the military to an extent that we are no longer able to provide sufficient training and management, we are inviting trouble.

The Issue of Nuclear Proliferation and Global Terrorism

Halting the spread of nuclear weapons and combating global terrorism are the issues that should be discussed together. Nuclear weapons are bad for our common security and for our common humanity, that is for sure. But if they are in the hands of responsible governments, we would have no justifiable reason to claim they are more dangerous than in the hands of our government. Furthermore, the purpose of American leadership in the world is to provide the common security to an extent that nuclear weapons, to the countries that hold them, are a liability instead of a tool. The goal must be to eliminate nuclear weapons from the planet altogether. It is seemingly difficult, but potentially possible. Think about the situation in a small village. If the village head has provided effective leadership that guaranteed common security, instead of bullying people around, how many ordinary villagers are willing to spend their precious resources and money to accumulate weapons? How useful are weapons in an orderly situation? If a villager suddenly starts stockpiling weapons, what reaction would he expect to receive from his fellow villagers? It is clear that in an orderly village, it is a very costly venture to stockpile dangerous weapons and very few people have the incentive to do so.

However, there are always some crazy people out there. Global terrorists are these people. I agree with Obama that "Because this enemy operates globally, it must be confronted globally."[15] As he quoted from a military commander: when people have dignity and opportunity, "the chance of extremism being welcomed greatly, if not completely, diminishes." He further proposed "to invest with our allies in strengthening weak states and helping to rebuild failed ones." Also, "combating the terrorists' prophets of fear will require more than lectures on democracy. . . . To empower forces of moderation, America must make every effort to export opportunity—access to education and health care, trade and investment—and provide the kind of steady support for political reformers and civil society that enabled our victory in the Cold War."[16] I believe these ideas are insightful. The globe is an organically connected whole. If we, as the leader, can facilitate an overall improvement of the whole, we will be able to, at least, minimize the individual problems. However, I would like to further emphasize that our focus should be on the connections with the right people instead of on being entangled with the wrong ones. Think about how the village head deals with trouble makers in his village. The most effective way for a village head to deal with a village trouble maker is not to come out into the open and fight fist to fist with him. A village head does not need to be physically stronger than the trouble maker. But he can mobilize a whole group of people to defeat him. The reason is simple, yet complex: he represents the whole village while the trouble maker hurts everybody, including himself.

In addition to the global vision, the village head must act locally. A key step for him to take is to develop close ties with these trouble makers' relatives and close friends. He must be with them socially as a friend, instead of an outsider or even an enemy. For many trouble makers, death is glory. The only people who can strike their hearts are the local people—the people they can related to. The only thing that can move them is the opposition of the people they feel close to. To apply the principle to anti-terrorism, we might be able to say: the key issue is how to build up effective connections to the local people.

In Afghanistan, five years after the American invasion, the Taliban is still there and is making inroads in some areas. This cannot be seen as a military issue alone. As foreigners, it is very difficult, if not impossible, for us to effectively connect to the local people. We must establish a government that can truly help us accomplish this task. Of course, we should help the Afghan government develop its military, its police force and its civil service. But we should look beyond the formal governmental constructions and never overlook the importance of the informal social ties the government operatives can develop with the local people. The government operatives must be present at all religious gatherings and social activities and become leaders in local people's social lives. People want good lives, want dignity and opportunity, that is true. But we must go some extra miles to localize the seemingly universal values. It is the informal social ties that define what is a good life, what is dignity and what is opportunity. Without social connections, the things we value dearly might not be worth much in the hearts of local people. We might think we offer them the opportunity of freedom—we make them speak their opinions freely, we organize free elections, we impose legal systems to guarantee their human rights, etc. But we might be surprised that the local people do not acknowledge the benefits that all of these bring to them. The informal social ties are the channel for us to reach people and to act locally.

I cannot agree with Obama's idea about Pakistan. Simply exerting more pressure on its current military government without taking the public sentiment into consideration will be counterproductive. We should facilitate the government with the capability to more effectively connect to its people instead of forcing it to cut off the connections. As in every society, there are many powerful and influential elements that play key roles in connecting the society and safeguarding the social fabric in Pakistan. We should help the government make connections to these elements in a socially constructive way. We must realize that only when we effectively connect to the local people can we benefit from the changeability of the minds and hearts of the local people.

Obama ended his discussion on the terrorism issue with an inspiring statement: "Our beliefs rest on hope; the extremists' rest on fear. This is why we can—and will—win this struggle."[17] I am sure we will win as long as our hope is grounded in effective connections and their fear is rooted in isolation.

The Issue of Homeland Security

As to the home front, I do not think the most important measure lies in the areas of technology or intelligence. It is in the local people—the same as anti-terrorism on the foreign front. We must rely on American people to defeat any terrorist attempt on our homeland. To transform this cliché into effective policy, we should act locally too. We should do whatever we can to overcome the issue of societal fragmentation. America was known as a melting pot, but it is no more. People have started saying that America is a salad bowl. It is descriptively true, but prescriptively harmful. I agree with Samuel Huntington that America as a society cannot sustain without societal coherence.[18] But it would not be effective if we follow his advice to force one religion, one ideology, and one language upon the whole society. The result would be too superficial on the one hand, and too divisive on the other. In the end, instead of constructing a coherent society, it will further fragment it. I would like to use a pot of soup as the metaphor to describe American society and to prescribe a way to make it more coherent. As we know, soup has one distinct taste, but each ingredient still, more or less, keeps its shape and characteristics. We must make every effort to develop connections across different social groups. The "weak tie" approach might be useful here. We need to push people to go out of their comfort zones to build up relationships with people who are different from themselves. The powerful and privileged groups of people especially need to do so. And all the groups must go through a process of transformation in the process of socially connecting to each other and therefore become a part of the overall system.

Alliances and Partnerships

Obama is insightful when he says "To renew American leadership in the world, I intend to rebuild the alliances, partnerships, and institutions necessary to confront common threats and enhance common security. Needed reform of these alliances and institutions will not come by bullying other countries to ratify changes we hatch in isolation."[19] But I think his solution is not adequate. According to him, the alliances and institutions "will come when we convince other governments and peoples that they, too, have a stake in effective partnerships."[20] But for me, the key is to make a sincere confession that we are limited and cannot do everything right. We need to develop relationships that share vulnerability. We can then involve others by respecting their appropriate roles in the structure of global system. So long as it is a partnership, we cannot act in a "my way or the highway" fashion. Obama did not mention that a leader in an alliance needs to adjust itself to its partners while leading. We are only part of the system, although a leading part. Our partners might not be the leading part, but they are indispensable to the system. We, together, work to safeguard the system.

Here, the connections are also important. We cannot assume other nations automatically recognize their stake in the common security system. Without a role to play in the system and without being effectively connected to the system, they might define their interests otherwise. The connectivist perspective views the alliances, partnerships, and international institutions as an entity to process and transform their individual members. It does not regard individual members as predetermined and already fully developed selves with a hard core that is unchangeable. Instead, it regards their national "selves" as fluid in a process of becoming. All transformations depend on whether the connections in which the actors are involved are tight enough. A leader is responsible to promote, stimulate, and facilitate this process for the benefit of the system as a whole. To accomplish this task, the leader itself must be ready to transform. This is the most important and most difficult task for the leader. I therefore do not agree with Obama's inspiring but harmful statement: "I will show the world that America remains true to its founding values."[21] If we believe this statement, we must regard our founding values as eternal and universal. If everyone in the alliances and partnerships and institutions attempts to show others it remains true to its founding values, it will not be possible for the system to process individual members and make them organic parts of the system. We will end up fighting the childish, useless and even harmful "who is right, who is wrong" battle. As the leader, we will not be able to make the system work in this way.

In fact, Obama sensed this point. When he talked about America's responsibility in protecting our environment, he mentioned many changes; some of them might lead to radical societal changes. That is the true leadership. If the system requires us to change, we just do it. We can then ask our partners and all others to do the same. We have to realize that change, even forced change, does not mean something bad. Just as Obama observed: "This challenge is massive, but rising to it will also bring new benefits to America."[22]

The Connection between Foreign Policy Formulation and Domestic Politics

I found it very inspiring to read Obama's words "There are compelling moral reasons and compelling security reasons for renewed American leadership that recognizes the inherent equality of worth of all people."[23] Yes, this should be the purpose of our leadership. But a difficult issue here is how we can reconcile this leadership orientation with local people's everyday concerns. Both at home and abroad, the government is not capable of reaching ordinary people without intermediaries. Even if we have the best intentions and unlimited resources, how can we guarantee our best intentions are not distorted and our resources are not abused? Here, what we need the most is not money, let alone rhetoric. Kennedy was right when he said, "If a free society cannot help the many who are poor, it cannot save the few who are rich." But in reality, we might have to go through the rich in order to help the poor. If we believe in capitalist private ownership and market economy and denounce communist state ownership and commanding economy, we would have to make every effort to encourage private investment, entrepreneurship and free trade in order for the capitalist forces to reach as many people as possible in a meaningful way. The whole purpose is to build up a system that is based on pushing the "haves" to effectively reach out to the "have-nots." If we talk up the top-down freedom, we would have to talk down the bottom-up equality.

The second major difficulty is how to balance the foreign and the domestic. Obama realized this difficulty by saying "Ultimately, no foreign policy can succeed unless the American people understand it and feel they have a stake in its success—unless they trust that their government hears their concerns as well."[24] His solution is to restore American people's trust in their president. This is a cliché without concrete and practical measures. Here we see the major conflict between an American style democratic political system and American global leadership.

The American style democracy is based on an assumption that each individual participates in the political process with her/his predestined interests. They therefore elect the leaders who can best represent their interests. This collective process does not change anything except producing a leader who can facilitate the fulfillment of people's predetermined wants and needs. However, in reality, all the individuals who participate in the political process, both the leaders and the voters, are changeable by the collective process. Their selves and their interests are created, shaped and reshaped by their interactions with each other and between the leaders and the led. As I pointed out in my previous book,[25] it is the embeddedness of formal political construction in informal ways of social ties that reflects the true nature of this

process. Since the original design of the American political system did not reflect the aspect of embeddedness, it lacks the strength to facilitate the social
connections between the political powerful and the less powerful or the powerless. People are free to choose their leaders in a secure environment without fear, but they have to do so with very limited choice and, especially, very
limited knowledge. Especially in the foreign policy area, the knowledge gap
between the politically powerful (the players/insiders) and the less powerful
(the spectators/outsiders) is huge. The formal system does not have the capability to bridge the gap. Only a new type of political system with emphasis on
social connections among all social groups can fill in the gap. The key issue
is empowerment of the spectators/outsiders by the players/insiders. I would
term this type as "connective democracy," which is the topic of Chapter 4.

A CONECTIVIST RESPONSE TO MITT ROMNEY

The Relationship between Theory and Policy

Romney began with a subtitle "Washington Divided." As he saw it, this
should not happen: "More broadly, lines have been drawn between those labeled 'realists' and those labeled 'neoconservatives.' Yet these terms means
little when even the most committed neoconservative recognizes that any successful policy must be grounded in reality and even the most hardened realist admits that much of the United State's power and influence stems from its
values and ideals."[26] But, theory does matter. It provides the fundamental orientation for a policy. First, different theories depict different views of the
world; second, they present different tasks for foreign policies to tackle.
Third, they supply different solutions. Realism depicts the world as anarchy.
Since everybody is out for themselves in an anarchic world, the major task for
foreign policy is to navigate through the power games. The solution therefore
is clear: the classic and neo-realism focus on balance of power and offensive
realism emphasizes being the strongest and the most powerful. When realists
talk about global leadership, they mean being a strong man with sufficient
strength to balance out others' power and guarantee the wants and needs of
the leader will be materialized.

Neoconservative perspective depicts the world with some degree of order—the order of market exchange, the order of international institutions, and
most importantly, the order of US dominated nation building. Their foreign
policy is therefore based on a hope—the hope of shaping the world in an
American way, with free trade market mechanism dominating the economies,
with the international institutions serving the needs of the US, and with
spreading democratic political system within nation-states as the means of a

US dominated mutual understanding and security guarantee. When the neoconservatives talk about global leadership, they mean being a global rule producer and order enforcer. Specifically, realists generally shy away from the task of nation-building while the neoconservatives actively seek the opportunity to do so.

Since "the share understanding of how to meet a new generation of challenge," around which a foreign policy is supposed to be constructed does not exist at all, a consistent theoretical guidance is necessary. Therefore, when Romney framed the United States' direction and role in the world, I would say he is essentially an offensive realist although he claimed that his formulation is "a new thinking on foreign policy and an overarching strategy that can unite the United States and its allies."[27]

The Issue of Leadership

Like Obama, Romney also talks about global leadership. But his notion of leadership is not about national leaders like Roosevelt, Truman and Kennedy. It is about "the greatest generation" of American people. Yes, it is true that "the greatest generation" accomplished amazingly in terms of constructing a better world. Romney listed the legacy of their accomplishments. But he did not mention an important fact: a nation with the highest level of human qualities may not automatically become a global leader. A global leader must be the one who is in the most favorable strategic position in the global structure and is best connected to all the significant others, as well as the generalized others, across the globe. The leadership role the US has been playing after World War II is more structural than individual. Here, the high level human quality and the best internal organizational system are the necessary conditions for the US to play this role. The sufficient condition was the special global structure after World War II with all the European nations at their weakest and Stalin's Soviet Union at its peak that bestowed the leadership role to the US. A bi-polar structure was a historical necessity. It is no doubt that "the greatest generation" seized the opportunity and lived up to the expectation of the others. We should also not overlook another structural factor—it was the capitalist world system that enabled "the greatest generation" to achieve the feat while the communist system failed the Soviet people.

At this point in history after the end of the Cold War, there is a tendency toward multi-polar global structure. The American led Iraqi War has highlighted this trend. As the only superpower, we failed to get support from most countries. We have been basically left alone to deal with the situation there—an embarrassing situation of a leader without followers. In the mean time, we have to realize that the communist system collapsed for good; everybody can potentially benefit from the energy generated by capitalist market economy and private investment. All the emerging powers are growing rapidly in terms of their individual strength and are becoming stronger in terms of their structural positions in the global system. This generation of American people is as great as the previous generations. But the American global leadership is challenged from all corners of the world. It is not because we are not as productive as previous generations; it is not because we are not as innovative and creative as previous generations. American ingenuity and entrepreneurship are alive and well; we are leading the world in space, technology, productivity, financial strength and military might. As an individual nation, we are as great as always. It is the new global structure of all nations that challenges this generation of American people about its global leadership role. Instead of promoting a historical nostalgia, we must think about this issue structurally and make ourselves functional in the new global system in order to keep our leadership position and play the role effectively.

The Iraqi Policy

Essentially, Romney wants the US troops to come home. But he wants them to be home after they get the job done. The reason is that "the stakes are too high and the potential fallout too great"[28] if they leave without forcing the warring factions of the Iraqi people into submission. It seems to me that his logic is as the followings: we have made a mess and we must clean it up before it gets worse. I believe I have illustrated my position clearly in my response to Obama and do not need to repeat it here. My only question is: How much worse can it be if we leave now? To me, the situation in and beyond Iraq is bad enough already. It is not likely to get any worse. On the contrary, it will have a chance to get better if we change our identity from an insider who is heavily entangled in the fighting to an outsider who is there to help. Do we have to fear the expansion of the Iranian influence? The answer seems clear: if we are in Iraq, Iran is the helper of the Iraqi Shiites who want American troops out. If we leave, Iran will become the enemy of the Iraqi people, Shiites and Sunnis alike, who have long been suspicious about the potential domination of the Iranians. Do we have to worry about al Qaeda operating in the Sunni area? I do not think so. If American troops are there, al Qaeda can get a legitimate reason to operate and can easily get support from the Sunni people. But once American troops leave, it is no longer a legitimate force. The rule of thumb is that the longer we stay, the more enemies we will make, and the harder it will be for our cause. The earlier we leave, the more friends we will get, and the better the chance for us to maintain our influence and power in that region.

The only concern I have is the Kurdish North of Iraq. The well developed Kurdish nationalism is a knotty issue because it might destabilize the border region between Turkey, Iraq, and Iran. But I think the US has the influence and power to resolve this issue. The US has been the guarantor and benefactor of the Kurdish people in Iraq since at least the first Golf War and it will play such a role in the future. Also, the Turkish military is a good friend of the US too. The effective connections we have with both parties have bestowed us with the leverage to pacify the situation. And more importantly, the Kurdish people have been benefiting from the economic growth of Turkey as a whole. In Istanbul, there are many Kurdish people who make a good living by actively participating in the economic activities in the majority Turk community. There is a high possibility that the Kurdish independent movement can be put on hold for as long as we need. In conclusion, I think Romney's worry is unfounded. The withdraw from Iraq will only produce good result rather than making us suffer bad consequences.

The Task and the Strategies

Islam is a civilization, a way of life. It is beyond national borders. I agree with Romney that we have to think globally in order to deal with the extremists inside Islam. Also, these people are organized differently. They live and operate in well connected networks. Their religious gatherings and their daily routine are mixed with their jihadist activities. We are not dealing with nation-states; we are not fighting with a professional army. This is indeed a new challenge. Romney's proposed change includes "four key pillars of action."

Strategy 1: Be Strong Militarily and Economically

First is the notion that you will never be wrong if you are strong. But Romney's only concrete proposal is to increase the military spending. Besides that, he proposes to enhance economic strength, but there is nothing new in his proposal.[29] As I mentioned before, being strong, or even the strongest, is far from being a leader. The essence of leadership is more structural than individual. Blindly developing strength without a strategic vision about how to put the strength in the appropriate structural position is simply wasting energy and resources. It may even be counterproductive in terms of leading. Before we decide to increase our spending on expanding the military, we must be very clear about two issues: first, what is the structural necessity on the global scale for us to use the stronger military; second, how are we supposed to use it in a functional and constructive way? I do not think Romney's proposal is clear on these two issues.

Strategy 2: Be Independent Energy-wise

His second idea is energy independence.[30] I agree with many of his proposals but I do not think the focus should be on energy "independence." It should be on how to be the global leader in the critical area of environmental utilization and protection. I therefore would like to add a connectivist construction to his proposal. The connectivist solution to the energy issue can be summarized in one sentence: be flexible; do what we are supposed to do based on our sensitivity to the environment. We must do what we are supposed to do instead of insisting on doing what we want to do. This is the only way for us to lead in the wake of a global environmental crisis. Currently we have two approaches to deal with environment and energy resources: the first is the attitude of plundering—we try our every means to seize and generate more energy and resources from nature; the second is the mechanism of market—the supply-demand relationship will naturally adjust to the usage of energy and resources. Connectivism would like to add another approach, I would term it the approach of oneness. The key question is: Do we have to use that much energy and resources? How can we possibly come up with new ways of living that do not need as much energy and as many resources? Here, the greatest generation's dedication and creativity will be at work. In the mean time, we would have to push for a fundamental change in the global structure of production and consumption.

It is very alarming to the United States that on the environmental issues, Germany is more and more taking the global leadership role while the US is becoming a distant follower. This is a good example for us and can lead us to think about how structural position and the functional role of individual members produce leaders, instead of an absolute volume of power that automatically makes the power holder a leader.

Strategy 3: Be More Effectively Organized

Romney's third proposal is creative and thought-provoking. He proposes unity among our international nonmilitary resources and organization of all the civilian agencies along common geographic boundaries with a clear line of authority. His model is the "joint command" system used to organize the military services on the regional bases. "For every region, one civilian leader should have authority over and responsibility for all the relevant agencies and departments, similar to the single military commander who heads U.S. Central Command."[31] From the connectivist perspective, this is not a good idea. The reason is that it is, in fact, copied from the organizational model of the multi-national corporations. As we all know, multi-national corporations send their teams of executives to certain regions and put them in charge of everything the company has in that region. However, this is an old-fashioned business model and has been abandoned for some time. The new business model is more consistent with the connectivist approach, which is termed as the global corporation model. The major difference between this model and the multi-national model is that the former incorporates the local people into its organization while the latter has to send its executive teams to the many countries they have business operations in. For global corporations, the majority of the leaders in their regional corporate headquarters are local people. They can far more effectively connect to the local resources, including financial capital, human capital, and especially social capital. On the contrary, the multi-corporation model cannot benefit much from this vital element of business operations. It has made "the mother" companies highly stretched. They have become exhausted because they have to spend their valuable management resources, as well as financial and social capital, in all the places that they have business operations. The "baby" companies have become the spending forces in most areas of the business operations (except the revenue and profit they might be able to generate, if the company is lucky and everything goes the right way).

Since Romney's proposal is so close to the multi-national corporation model, I would say it is better to modify it into the global corporation model. It is, of course, no small task to implement this model in international politics, but the connectivist approach has pointed to a highly effective way of organizing. It is at least a direction that is worthwhile to attempt.

Strategy 4: Be Multilateral the American Way

I share Romney's view that "the United States is stronger when its friends stand alongside it."[32] We cannot surrender because of some setbacks with the international community and withdraw into unilateralism.

However, I disagree with Romney on his view about the United Nations and some other international organizations.[33] It is true that the United Nations seems to not be as effective as many people would like it to be. But it is not fair or truthful to blame the United Nations as an organization. The reason for its ineffectiveness is clear: the major world powers, especially the United States, use it only as a tool for their own purposes. They do not respect it as an independent aggregate with a distinctive organizational pursuit. At a very least, the United Nations represents global sentiments; it is a forum on which the crosscurrents of all global forces meet. We cannot expect it to be a super government or the government of the world. From the connectivist perspective, it is just right for it to be this way. It is loose enough for its individual members to freely connect to each other through it; it is tight enough to legitimize its members' existence and facilitate the formation of collective sentiments across the globe.

It is a place to display the common humanity in its practical and collective form, as it is opposed to the ideal form defined solely by individual members. As a global leader, instead of single mindedly constructing our national interests in isolation and then forcing these wrongly conceived national interests upon the United Nations, we must be keenly aware of the structural function of the United Nations and use it effectively to facilitate our global leadership. And in the mean time, we must be ready to be changed, from the construction of our national interests to our actions safeguarding them, by our involvement with this international organization.

It is unfortunate that Romney did not recognize this point. His proposal has a strong flavor of the defamed "coalition of the willing." Even when he talked about the NATO alliance, he did not mention at all about how to adjust ourselves and how to involve others. According to the connectivist view, whenever we talk about alliance, we do not simply regard it as a tool for us to accomplish our goal or to make us stronger. We must recognize the powerful collective mechanism of any alliance that shapes its participant members and be ready to adjust ourselves in order to lead the operation of the alliance. If we want an alliance to be successful and want to be an effective leader of it, we must know that we are a part of a collective entity—we are one aspect of a whole. This is the most effective way for us to connect to others in the alliance and be a leader.

As I mentioned when I responded to Obama's proposal, the best way for a village head to deal with the troublesome "jihadists" in his village is to forge close ties (alliance) with their relatives and close friends. If all the parents and close relatives of the "jihadists" support the idea of putting them in jail or forcefully sending them for re-education, the task of minimizing the jihadists' destructive behavior would be much easier. By the same logic, to deal with the real jihadists, we would have to forge alliances with all the Islamic forces that oppose the extremists. Again, we have to be aware that we do not set out to use these people as tools for our purpose. We work with them together for a common purpose and we are ready to do what we are supposed to do as we ask them to do what they are supposed to do. No individuality or predetermined interests or character need to be safeguarded, as long as we focus on the common goal of defeating the jihadists.

Based on this connectivist understanding, I do not think Romney's concrete proposals are the most effective ones. It is true that "A growing population and a lack of jobs create fertile ground for radical Islam."[34] But it is far from the whole picture. In many other places across the globe, people are poor, even poorer than the people in Arabic countries, but they do not develop anti-American sentiment. They do not engage in terrorist activities. A Marshall Plan like economic revival project might be too costly for its limited results today. Romney proposed to create "a Partnership for Prosperity and Progress: a coalition of states that would assemble resources from developed nations and use them to support public schools (not Wahhabi madrasahs), microcredit and banking, the rule of law, human rights, basic health care, and free market policies in modernizing Islamic states." He believes that "new trade and economic opportunities for the Middle East. . . could be powerful forces."[35]

This proposal will only work if it follows the principle of connectiveness. Only when economic prosperity and sufficient modern education can generate social connections between the local people, at least the leaders of the local people, and the United States, can these measures be effective in defeating the jihadists. We have to be cautious that free market force is not necessarily a force of connection. It might be able to connect some people who can effectively participate in the free trade activities. But it runs the risk of further alienating the people who do not have the means or ability to be part of the market system. Market force has the potential to create huge gaps between the system insiders and the outsiders and therefore divide the society further. The alienated outsiders will become even more destructive and the conflict will be even more intensified. The institutionalization of the market economy and a legal society must be embedded in rich social connections. Otherwise, the social dynamics created by this change might be even more harmful to America's global leadership, as well as to a peaceful world.

We have been talking about changing "the hearts and minds of hundreds of millions of Muslims" for a long time. It is true that they need to change and they will be changed for better if the right global structure and functional connections are established. However, we also need to talk about changing our own hearts and minds. For the purpose of better preparing us to be the leader that can lead the hundreds of millions of Muslims out of the potentially dangerous trap set by the jihadists, we must be ready to change, to adjust, and to be flexible and sensitive to the structural necessities. We might have to adjust ourselves to the functional role we are supposed to play, not to simply maintain the way we are and do what we like.

"Moving Forward"

It is true that historically "confronting challenges has always made the United States stronger."[36] However, it is important to note that it is the structural force and the functional connection that made this possible. The new challenge requires us to continuously play a functional role as the global leader and this role requires us to reshape who we are by relating to what we are supposed to do. Despite all the discussions and rhetoric about the uniqueness of American character, "the greatest generation" in American history displayed a high level of flexibility with perseverance. Unlike Romney, I disagree with Shimon Peres when he said America "laid down hundreds of thousands of lives of its own sons and daughters and asked for nothing for itself."[37] It was true that we did not take land from either Germany or Japan, but we established a global system that has lasted until today. This system serves as a structure that has greatly benefited America and advanced its national interests. This global system has benefited us much, much more than a piece of land we could have been able to take from Germany or Japan. "The greatest generation" had the vision and dedication to adjust themselves to fit into the leadership positions in the structure that was built under their leadership. I therefore disagree with Romney that it is not because we are a unique nation so there is no substitute for our leadership. Only if we do not see ourselves as unique and we adjust ourselves to the role we are supposed to play in the new global structure in a timely fashion, can we be the global leader and better advance our national interests.

TOWARD A RELATIONSHIP ORIENTED FOREIGN POLICY

It is well known that the Machiavellian formula of power can be constructed as:

Power = lion (strength—military and economic power) + fox (wisdom— diplomacy).

The contemporary foreign policy constructions about global leadership, realism and idealism alike, have not gone beyond this formula much. Its key ingredients are hard power, soft power, plus international institutions. Hence, the currently dominant foreign policy orientation for global leadership can be stated as the following:

To be a global leader is to play a role as the rule-enforcer based on maximizing national power in an international system of power struggle—being the strongest (realism) and the most attractive (idealism) and exercising both of these cleverly through establishing and enforcing favorably constructed legal and normative systems.

However, based on the construction of connective authority, the connectivist formula of power can be constructed as:

Global Connective Power = wolf (well positioned functional connection and relational connection) + lion (strong military and economic strength) + fox (smart diplomacy)

Here, power and global leadership are embedded in legitimacy in the inclusive webs of functional and relational connections. Power and leadership are not "things" out there—they only become real in the dynamic process of being a part of a functional- relational web. Leadership is "power with" instead of "power over". In the mean time, it is not about appeasement or unprincipled accommodation. It is about the way through which the strong are enabled and the weak are empowered. Therefore, the connectivist formula for global leadership can be formulated as the following:

*Global Leadership = connective authority (instrumental and inclusion) * (hard power + soft power)*

Based on this formula, a global leader is a village head. Its powers can only be multiplied by its connective authority. It exercises its leadership through positioning itself instrumentally in the global structure, weaving relational webs of connections and building inclusive, flexible and authoritative international legal and normative institutions. To individual nation-states that have the hard and soft power to play the global leadership role, this is not an easy task. The difficulty is less in the complexity of getting so many different individual power players together, organizing them, shaping their agendas, transforming them into effective members of the global village, and making them work together toward a common good, and more about the unwillingness of the most powerful players in the international scene to minimize their "big egos", give up their "my way or the highway" mentalities, and stop unilaterally constructing national interests without contextual and relational perspectives.

It is true that politically and economically, we are in an anarchic world—each nation-state has to look after its own interests; everybody is out for him or herself. The two major schools in the field of international studies are sound based on this assumption: balance of power is important, distribution of capability is critical, economic interdependence is the foundation and normative construction is anything but soft. The Westphalian sovereign nation-state system is still alive and well. The unit of action in international relations is still nation-states. However, socially, the international system of power distribution is clear: in this 192 nation-states global village, the fundamental mechanism is togetherness: we are together no matter how hard we struggle to detach from each other. We live in an inescapable and tightly knit social unit and we have to stay on this planet without any other choice. We are bound together tightly by the very fact that we have no way of escaping from each other! We hold each other hostage, as a Buddhist might say. Therefore, we share vulnerability. We are weak one way or another—not because human beings are not capable of dealing with natural disasters, but because we have to face the daily possibility of hurting each other if we are not capable of keeping relationships between or among us.

However, the dialectic relationship between structure and agency is also clear: not everybody knows their best interests and acts upon them. Nation-states are more likely than not to be driven by their drive for misconceived national glory, narrowly constructed national interests, and wrongly positioned senses of power. Just as individuals often do something destructive to their own, nation-states, under the domination of the elite groups, are likely to do the same. To avoid this destructive action from happening, nation-states must match their active efforts to the global structure. It might be inevitable for conquest to occur; it might be natural for nation-states to develop systems of interdependence by including their own and excluding all others that are viewed as undependable. But powerful nation-states that have the potential to play a leadership role in global affairs must drive for connection. This is the only way they can make their power constructive and meaningful. It is fair to say that they have gone a long way and have achieved so much. But most of the time they did it unconsciously without realizing the theoretical framework behind what they were doing. Their frame of thinking is limited in the "lion + fox" box, which regards connection and collective power dynamics as normative gestures instead of necessities. Diplomacy, therefore, becomes an exercise of foxing tactics instead of applying wolfingly connective and collective strategies. We have learned enough lessons. As smart human beings, we should consciously realize our best interests and act upon them. Only through working together can we survive individually.

NOTES

1. T. D. Jakes, "The World's Pulse," *Atlantic Monthly*, the 150th anniversary issue, (2007): 36.

2. Anne-Marie Slaughter, "Unexceptionalistm," *Atlantic Monthly*, the 150th anniversary issue, (2007): 50.

3. Talcott Parsons, Robert F. Bales, and Edward A Shils, *Working Papers in the Theory of Action* (Glencoe, Ill. Free Press, 1953).

4. Robert D. Putnam, *Bowling Alone: the collapse and revival of American Community* (New York: Simon and Schuster, 2000); Nan Lin, *Social Capital—a theory of social structure and action* (New York: Cambridge University Press, 2001).

5. Barack Obama, "Renewing American Leadership," *Foreign Affairs*, (July/August 2007); Mitt Romney, "Rising to a New Generation of Global Challenges," *Foreign Affairs*, (July/August 2007).

6. Obama, 3–4.

7. Obama, 4/5.

8. Obama, 4.
9. Obama, 4.
10. Obama, 2.
11. Obama, 4.
12. Obama, 4.
13. Obama, 4.
14. Obama, 5–6.
15. Obama, 9.
16. Obama, 11.
17. Obama, 11.
18. Samuel Huntington, *Who Are We? The Challenges to America's National Identity* (New York: Simon & Shuster, 2004).
19. Obama, 11.
20. Obama, 11.
21. Obama, 13.
22. Obama, 13.
23. Obama, 15.
24. Obama, 15.
25. Tian-jia Dong, Understanding Power through Watergate (Lanham, MD: University Press of America, 2005): 136–138.
26. Romney, 17.
27. Romney, 18.
28. Romney, 20.
29. Romney, 23–25.
30. Romney, 25–26.
31. Romney, 26–27.
32. Romney, 28.
33. Romney, 28–29.
34. Romney, 29.
34. Romney, 30.
34. Romney, 32.
34. Romney, 32.

Bibliography

Arblaster, Anthony. *Democracy,* Minneapolis: University of Minnesota Press, 1987

Blumer, Herbert. "Society as Symbolic Interaction," in Arnold Rose (ed.), *Human Behavior and Social Processes*, New York: Houghton Mifflin, 1962

Burke, Edmund. *Reflections on the Revolution in France*, Harmondsworth: Penguin Book, 1968

Burt, Ronald. *Toward a Structural Theory of Action: Network Models of Social Structure, Perception and Action,* New York: Academic Press, 1982

———. *Structure Holes; the social structure of competition*, Cambridge, MA: Harvard University Press, 1992

Coleman, James. *Community Conflict*, Glencoe Ill.: Free Press, 1957

Collins, Randall. *Conflict Sociology*, New York: Academic Press, 1975

Cook, Karen S. "Exchange and Power in Networks of Interorganizational Relations," *Sociological Quarterly,* No. 18, Winter 1977

Cook, Karen S. and Richard Emerson. "Power, Equity and Commitment in Exchange Networks," *American Sociological Review,* Vol. 43, 1978

Cook, Karen S. Richard M. Emerson, Mary R. Gillmore, and Toshio Yamagish. "The Distribution of Power in Exchange Networks," *American Journal of Sociology*, Vol. 89, 1983

Cook, Karen S. and Karen A. Hegtvedt. "Distributive Justice, Equity, and Equality," *American Sociological Review* 39, 1983

Coser, Lewis. *The Function of Social Conflict,* London: Free Press of Glencoe, 1956

Crick, Bernard. *In Defense of Politics*, London: Weidnenfeld & Nicolson, 1962

Dahl, Robert. "The Concept of Power," *Behavioral Science* 2, 1957

———. *Dilemmas of Pluralist Democracy*, London: Yale University Press, 1982

Dahrendorf, Ralf. "Out of Utopia: Toward a Reorientation of Sociological Analysis," American Journal of Sociology 64, September, 1958

Dewey, John and Arthur F. Bentley, *Knowing and the Known*, in *Useful procedures of Inquiry,* edited by Rollo Handy and E.C. Harwood, Behavior Research Council, Great Barrington, MA, 1973

DiMaggio, Paul and Hugh Louch. "Social Embedded Consumer Transactions: for what kinds of purchases do people most often use networks?" *American Sociological Review* 63, October 1998

Dong, Tian-jia. *Understanding Power through Watergate: the Washington collective power dynamics,* Lanham, MD: University Press of America, 2005

Doyle, Michael. "Liberalism and World Peace," *American Political Science Review* 80 (4): 1151–69, 1986

Durkheim, Emile. *The Division of Labor in Society*, trans. G. Simpson, New York: Free Press, 1964

Emerson, Richard. "Power-Dependence Relations," *American Sociological Review,* 17, Feb. 1962,

———. "Power-Dependence Relations: Two Experiments," *Sociometry,* 27 Sept. 1964

Euripides. *The Suppliant Women*, in Orestes and other plays, trans. Philip Vellancott, Harmondsworth: Penguin Book, 1972

Farrand, Max. ed. The Records of the Federal Convention of 1787, vols. I–III, New Haven, CT.: Yale University Press, 1966

Fraser, Steve and Gary Gerstle, ed. *Ruling America: A History of Wealth and Power in a Democracy,* Cambridge, MA: Harvard University Press, 2005

Fukuyama, Francis. *The End of History and the Last Man,* New York: Free Press, 1992

Gamson, William. *The Strategy of Social Protest*, Homewood, Ill,: Dorsey Press, 1975

Gaubatz, Kurt. "Democratic States and the Commitment in International Relations," *International Organization* 50:1 (1996): 109–39

Geertz, Clifford. "On the Nature of Anthropological Understanding," *American Scientist:* 63, 1975

Green, Peter. *A concise History of Ancient Greece*, London: Thames & Hudson, 1973

Anderson, Perry. *Passages From Antiquity to Feudalism*, London: New Left Books, 1974, Hamilton, Alexander, James Madison, and John Jay, *The Federalist,* with the Letters of "Brutus." Ed. Terence Ball, Cambridge UK.: Cambridge University Press, 2003

Huntington, Samuel. "The Democratic Distemper," The Public Interest 39, Spring 1975

———. *The Clash of Civilizations and the Remaking of World Order,* New York: A Touchstone Book, 1996

———. *Who Are We? The Challenges to America's National Identity*, New York: Simon & Shuster, 2004

Ikenberry, John. *After Victory: Institutions, Strategic Restraints and the Rebuilding of Order after Wars,* Princeton, NJ: Princeton University Press, 2001

Jakes, T. D. "The World's Pulse", *Atlantic Monthly*, the 150th anniversary issue, 2007

Jefferson, Thomas. "Notes on the State of Virginia," in *The Portable Thomas Jefferson,* ed. Merrill D. Peterson, Harmondsworth: Penguin Books, 1977

Jervis, Robert. "Cooperation under the Security Dilemma," *World Politics*, Vol. 30, No. 2, January 1978.

Johnson, Steven. *Humanizing the Narcissistic Style.* New York: W.W. Norton, 1987

Keohane, Robert O. *Neorealism and Its Critics*, ed. New York: Columbia University Press, 1986

———. *After Hegemony: Cooperation and Discord in the World Political Economy*, Princeton, NJ: Princeton University Press, 1984

———. "Theory of World Politics: Structural Realism and Beyond," in Ada W. Finifter, ed., *Political Science: The State of the Discipline*, Washington, D.C.: American Political Science Association, 1983

Kornhauser, William. *The Politics of Mass Society,* London: Routledge & Kegan Paul, 1960

Krugman, Paul. *The Great Unravelling: Losing Our Way in a New Century,* New York, NY.: W.W. Norton & Company, 2003

Lawrence, D. H. "Democracy," in *Selected Essays,* Harmondsworth, Penguin Books, 1950

Leeds, Brett Ashley. "Democratic Political Institutions, Credible Commitments, and International Cooperation," *American Journal of Political Science* 43 (4): 979–1002, 1999

Lin, Nan. *Social Capital—a theory of social structure and action,* New York: Cambridge University Press, 2001

Lippmann, Walter. *The Public Philosophy*, New York: Mentor Books, 1956

Lipset, S. M. *Political Man,* London: Heinemann, 1960

Lipson, Charles. *Reliable Partners*, Princeton: Princeton University Press, 2003

Lockwood, David. "Some Remarks on 'The Social System." *British Journal of Sociology* 7, June 1956

Macpherson, C. B. *The Real World of Democracy*, Oxford: Clarendon Press, 1966

Granovetter, Mark. "The Strength of Weak Ties" *American Journal of Sociology* 78, No.6, 1973

———. "Economic Action and Social Structure: the problem of embeddedness" *American Journal of Sociology* 91, No.3, 1985

———. "The Theory-Gap in Social Network Analysis," in Paul Holland and Samuel Leinhardt, eds. *Perspectives on Social Network Research,* New York: Academic Press, 1979

———. "The Strength of Weak Ties: A Network Theory Revisited," *Sociological Theory*, No.1, 1983

Markus, Hazel and S. Kitayama. "Culture and the Self: implications for cognition, emotion, and motivation." *Psychological Review* Vol. 98, No.2, 1991

Marsden, Peter and Nan Lin. eds.,*Social Structure and Network Analysis*, Beverly Hills, CA.: Sage Publications, 1982

Marx, Karl and Friedrich Engels. *Manifesto of the Communist Party,* in *The Marx-Englels Reader*, second edition, ed. Robert C. Tucker, New York: W.W Norton, 1978

Mearsheimer, John. *The Tragedy of Great Power Politics,* New York: W.W. Norton, 2001

Mill, James. *Utilitarian Logic and Politics*, ed. Jack Lively and John Rees, Oxford: Clarendon Press, 1978

Morgenthau, Hans J. *Politics Among Nations*, seventh edition, Boston: McGraw Hill, 2006

Morris, Robert B. ed. *Alexander Hamilton and the Founding of the Nation*, New York: Harper Torchback, 1969

Nye Jr., Joseph. *Soft Power: The Means to Success in World Politics,* New York: Public Affairs, 2004

————. *Bound to Lead, The Changing Nature of American Power,* New York: Basic Books, 1990.

Obama, Barack. "Renewing American Leadership," *Foreign Affairs*, July/August 2007

Ohmae, Kenichi. *Borderless World: power and strategy in the interlinked economy,* (revised edition), New York: HarperBusiness, 1999

Owen, John. "How Liberalism Produces the Democratic Peace," *International Security,* 19 (2): 87–125, 1994

Oye, Kenneth A. ed. *Cooperation under Anarchy,* Princeton, NJ: Princeton University Press, 1985

Thomas. Paine, *Common Sense,* Harmondsworth, Penguin Books, 1976

Parsons, Talcott "The Present Position and Prospect of Systemic Theory in Sociology." *Essays in Sociological Theory,* New York: Free Press, 1949

————. *Social System,* New York: Free Press, 1951

————. *Action Theory and The Human Condition,* New York: Free Press, 1978

Parsons, Talcott, Robert F. Bales, and Edward A Shils, *Working Papers in the Theory of Action,* Glencoe, Ill. Free Press, 1953

Plato, Protagoras, in *Protagoras and Meno,* trans. W.K.C. Guthrie, Harmondsworth, Penguin Books, 1956

Przeworski, Adam, Susan C. Stokes, and Bernard Manin, ed. *Democracy, Accountability, and Representation.* Cambridge, UK: Cambridge University Press, 1999

Putnam, Robert D. *Bowling Alone: the collapse and revival of American Community,* New York: Simon and Schuster, 2000

Qin, Dongxiao. "Toward a Critical Feminist Perspective of Culture and Self," *Feminism & Psychology,* Vol. 14, No. 2, 2004

Ray, James. *Democracy and International Conflict,* Columbia: University of South Carolina Press, 1995

Romney, Mitt. "Rising to a New Generation of Global Challenges," *Foreign Affairs,* July/August 2007

Rousseau, Jean-Jacques. *Du Contrat Social,* Book IV, Ch. 2. In Anthony Arblaster, *Democracy,* Minneapolis: University of Minnesota Press, 1987

Russett, Bruce. *Grasping the Democratic Peace,* Princeton: Princeton University Press, 1993

Schumpeter, Joseph. *Capitalism, Socialism and Democracy,* London: George Allen & Unwin, 1943

Scott, John. *Social Network Analysis—a handbook,* second edition, London: Sage Publications, 2000

Shelling, Thomas C. *The Strategy of Conflict,* Cambridge MA: Harvard University Press, 1960

Simmel, Georg. *Conflict and the Web of Group Affiliation,* trans. Kurt H. Wolff and Reinhard Bendix, New York: Free Press, 1955

————. *The Philosophy of Money,* Boston: Routledge & Kegan Paul, 1978

————. "Faithfulness and Gratitude," in Kurt Wolff, ed. and trans., *The Sociology of Georg Simmel,* New York: Free Press, 1950

Skocpol, Theda. *Diminished Democracy: from membership to management in American civil life.* Norman: University of Oklahoma Press, 2003

Slaughter, Anne-Marie. "Unexceptionalistm", *Atlantic Monthly*, the 150th anniversary issue, 2007

Stinchcombe, Arthur L. *Constructing Social Theories*, New York: Hartcourt, Brace, & World, 1968

Stolte, John F. and Richard M. Emerson, "Structural Inequality: Position and Power in Network Structures," in *Behavioral Theory in Sociology*, ed. R. Hamblin, New Brunswick, N.J.: Transaction Book, 1977

Thucydides. *The Peloponnesian War,* trans. John Warrington, London: Dent Everyman, 1959

Turner, Jonathan H. *The Structure of Social Theory,* fourth edition, Chicago, Ill. The Dorsey Press, 1986

Walder, Andrew. *Communist Neo-Traditionalism*, Berkeley, CA: University of California Press, 1986

Waltz, Kenneth N. *Man, the State, and War: A Theoretical Analysis*, New York: Columbia University Press, 1959;

——. *Theory of International Politics*, Reading, MA: Addison-Wesley, 1979

Weber, Max. *The Theory of Social and Economic Organizations*, trans. by A.M. Henderson and Talcott Parsons, New York: Oxford University Press, 1947

——. *Economy and Society*, Cambridge, MA: Harvard University Press, 1954

——. *From Max Weber: essays in sociology,* (paperback edition), Hans H. Gerth and C. Wright Mills, eds., New York: Oxford University Press, 1958

Wellman, Berry. "Network Analysis: Some Basic Principles," *Sociological Theory*, 1, 1983

Index

acceptability, 45
accommodation, 115
acculturation, 14
adaptation, 24, 95
Afghanistan, 102
Africa, 85
al Qaeda, 108
alienation, 18, 74, 83, 85, 113
allegiances, local, 79
Alliance for Progress, 97
American: character, 113; democracy
(*see* democracy); hegemony, x;
identity, 93 (*see also* cultural identity
and national identity); leadership, 45,
96, 101, 103; global leadership, 105
Americans, 70
anarchic world, the, 115
anarchy, 1, 2, 5, 7, 20, 106
anti-American sentiment, 112
anti-terrorism, 102–3
appeasement, 115
Arabic countries, 112
Arblaster, Anthony, 79–80
aristocracy, 83
Aristotle, 81
association: social, 27 (*see also*
connectedness); sectional, 74
Athenian System, 76, 78. *See also*
democracy

authority, 49; charismatic, 47, 49–50,
61, 64; connective, vi, 42, 46,
47–49, 66, 88, 114–15; formal
construction of, 55; global, 46;
inclusive, 62, 69 (*see also* authority
of inclusion); instrumental, 53–56,
62, 69 (*see also* authority of
instrumentation); rational/legal, 47,
49–50, 55, 63–64; relational, ix;
three ideal types of, 47–49, 63–64;
traditional, 47, 49, 51, 62, 64;
transactional, x; types of, 61
authority of: inclusion, 19, 57–61–64,
71; of instrumentation, 19, 52, 57,
61–64, 71

balance theory, psychological, x,
balance of power, 2, 40, 98, 106, 115
beacon of hope, 46
bi-polar structure, 107
Blumer, Herbert, 3
bonding, 31, 89. *See also* social ties
bonds, durable, 3. *See also* social ties
borderless institutions, 12
bottom-up: approach, 81, 86; force, 18
bourgeoisie, interest-based, 27
bridging, 31, 89. *See also* social ties
bureaucracy, 51
Burk, Edmund, 75, 82

Westphalian sovereign nation-state
    system, 2, 115 (*see also* sovereignty
    will); connective (*see* connective
    will); general (*see* general will); of
    all, 73, 86; of majority, 86
will or interest formation, 86

Wilson, Woodrow, 84
working class, 30
world: governance (*see* governance);
    government, 1, 66, 70; society, 70
    (*see also* global village and
    community)